WORD STUDIES
9Ed

Devern J. Perry
Professor of Management Communications
Brigham Young University

South-Western
Educational Publishing

Project Manager: Laurie Wendell
Editor: Marianne Miller
Cover Design: Tin Box Studio
Internal Design: Paul Neff
Marketing Manager: Carolyn Love

ISBN: 0–538–71274–0

1 2 3 4 5 6 BN 00 99 98 97 96 95

Printed in the United States of America

I(T)P
International Thomson Publishing Company

South-Western Educational Publishing is a division of International Thomson Publishing Inc. The ITP trademark is used under license.

PREFACE

As you use *Word Studies,* 9th Edition, you will grow in confidence and in your ability to use and spell words correctly. This book takes a positive approach to systematically building skill upon skill.

As you complete the activities in this book, you will

- use the dictionary and thesaurus effectively

- overcome difficulties with troublesome words

- apply prefixes and suffixes to root words

- employ plural and possessive forms of nouns

- master new words and use synonyms and antonyms for new and for frequently used words

- learn computer-related and business-related terminology

MAJOR CHANGES

Word Studies, 9th Edition, has been completely rewritten and presents a number of major changes, for example:

- The **thesaurus** is discussed along with the dictionary as a valuable tool for learning new words.

- **Business-related vocabularies** and **computer-related vocabularies** have been incorporated as small units into each part, allowing you to learn business and computer words as you progress.

- **Activities** no longer focus on word lists to teach concepts, but rely on contextual clues to allow answer discovery.

- **Part 7**, entirely new to this edition, reviews the contents of Parts 1 through 6, spelling words, word pairs, business-related terminology, and computer-related terminology.

Review Exercises

The end-of-part review exercises have been completely revised, and new review exercises have been placed at the midpoint of each part. This midway review allows you to check your learning and see if you need additional assistance before continuing. These exercises may be used as a review, a self-text, or a more formalized examination of your learnings. Each part also contains a review of the special word lists presented in the activities. These may be used as reviews or self-tests.

Additionally, an inventory test, six achievement tests, and a final examination are available to users of this text.

ACKNOWLEDGMENTS

Special thanks to all the instructors who have used previous editions of *Word Studies* and provided helpful feedback. Thanks also to the following reviewers of this new edition for their guidance and expertise:

Joan Cone, El Cerritto High School, Richmond, CA

Joseph Lee, Horry-Georgetown Technical College, Conway, SC

Mary Moody, Pioneer Pacific College, Tigard, OR

Rhonda Wilson, Palm Beach Gardens High School, West Palm Beach, FL

BEST RESULTS

You will obtain results as you study each rule, guideline, and word presented in the text. Give new words and words that cause you difficulty special attention. Make a practice of studying these words in detail in the lesson and in later reviews. As you study and apply each word, you make that word *your own*.
Devern J. Perry

CONTENTS

PART 1 Using Your References: The Dictionary and the Thesaurus 1

PART 2 Working with Words 19

PART 3 Prefixes 37

PART 4 Suffixes 59

PART 5 Plurals and Possessives 85

PART 6 Synonyms and Antonyms 101

PART 7 Review Exercises 117

References 129

USING YOUR REFERENCES: THE DICTIONARY AND THE THESAURUS

Using the Dictionary		2
Activity 1	Identifying Syllables	5
Activity 2	Identifying Parts of Speech	6
Activity 3	Identifying Words with Two Pronunciations	7
	The Dictionary: Review	8
	Using the Thesaurus	9
	Using the Computerized Thesaurus	10
Activity 4	Using the Thesaurus	11
Activity 5	Using the Thesaurus for Synonyms and Antonyms	12
Activity 6	Spelling Words Correctly—Set 1	13
Activity 7	Making Sense of Word Pairs—Set 1	14
Activity 8	Business-Related Terminology—Set 1	15
Activity 9	Computer-Related Terminology—Set 1	16
	The Dictionary and Thesaurus: Review	17
	Special Word Lists: Review	18

Part

Using the Dictionary

When you meet with an old friend, you can relax and take off your shoes. You can trust your friend to be there for you, to be dependable, to help. An old friend is always available in times of need.

Although this old friend is most likely a person or an animal, you may also feel very comfortable with a good book. In this sense, you might consider a dictionary or other reference tool an old friend. With a dictionary, you can relax, knowing your dependable friend is there to help.

For many of us, however, the dictionary is used only as a last resort. When told to check the dictionary for the spelling of a particular word, some reply, "If I could look up the word, I'd know how to spell it!" As you become more comfortable and familiar with your dictionary, you will discover it to be a valuable resource, a good friend.

Before reading further, take the following pretest to see how well you know your dictionary.

Directions: *The illustration of the dictionary entry is from the* Thorndike-Barnhart Student Dictionary *and shows colored lines and numbers pointing to various dictionary parts. Locate the identified part in the following list and write the corresponding number from the illustration on the appropriate blank.*

_____ accent mark _____ definition _____ guide words

_____ main entry _____ part of speech _____ pronunciation

_____ singular form _____ subentry _____ syllable

① **country** | **courtier** ⑥ ⑧

② **coun try** (kun′trē), *n., pl.* **-tries,** adj. —*n.* **1** land, region, or district: *The country around the mining town was rough and hilly.* **2** all the land of a nation. **3** land where a person was born or is a citizen. **4** people of a nation. **5** land outside of cities and towns; rural district. **6** the public; the body of voters. —*adj.* **1** of the country; in the country; rural. **2** like the country. [< Old French *contree* < Medieval Latin *contrata* region lying opposite < Latin *contra* against]

⑨

⑮ **country club,** club in the country near a city. It has a clubhouse and facilities for outdoor sports.

③ **country cousin,** a countrified relative pleased but confused by things in the city.

coun try-dance (kun′trē dans′), *n.* dance in which partners face each other in two long lines.

coun try fied (kun′trē fīd), *adj.* countrified.

⑭ ⑤

④ the bond and presented for payment. [< French < *couper* to cut] —**cou′pon less,** *adj.* ⑦ ⑬

cour age (ker′ij), *n.* **1** meeting danger without fear; bravery; fearlessness. See synonym study below. **2 have the courage of one's convictions,** act as one believes one should. [< Old French *corage* < *cuer* heart < Latin *cor*]

⑩ **Syn. 1 Courage, bravery** mean fearlessness. **Courage** applies to moral strength that makes a person face any danger, trouble, or pain steadily and without showing fear: *The pioneer women faced the hardships of the westward trek with courage.* **Bravery** applies to a kind of courage that is shown by bold, fearless, daring action in the presence of danger: *They owed their lives to the bravery of the fireman.* ⑪

cou ra geous (kə rā′jes), *adj.* full of courage; brave; fearless. See **brave** for synonym study. —**cou ra′geous ly,** *adv.*

⑫

IDENTIFIED PARTS OF THE DICTIONARY

The following parts of the dictionary and their corresponding numbers are illustrated on page 2.

1. **Guide Words:** (**country** and **courtier**) Guide words are printed at the top of each page and indicate the span of words contained on that page or on facing pages. The word on the left, *country*, indicates the first word on the page, and the word on the right indicates either the last word on the page or the last word on the right-hand page.

2. **Main Entry:** (**country**) The main entry is the word to be pronounced and defined. It appears in a bolder print than the other words in the entry. Main entries may appear as single-word entries (**courage**), compound-word entries (**countryfied**—circled number 14), phrase entries (**country club**—circled number 15), abbreviation entries (**bx**), and letter-of-the-alphabet entries (**C** and **c**).

3. **Subentry:** (**country cousin**) A subentry is a word or expression that uses the main-entry word but has a special meaning of its own, often unrelated to that of the main entry. The subentry often appears in boldface type; it is generally placed within the definition of the main entry rather than at the margin, as has been done in the illustration on page 2. Other examples of subentries for other words are **on the money** (main entry: **money**) and **pull out all the stops** (main entry: **stop**).

4. **Syllable:** (**cour** in **courage**) A syllable is any part of a word pronounced as a unit. Most dictionaries break the main entry into syllables; for example, **cour age** and **coun try**.

5. **Accent Mark:** (kun′ trē and dans′) The accent mark indicates the syllable receiving the emphasis, or stress, in pronunciation. Primary stress is indicated by the primary mark: (′). When secondary stress is shown, the accent mark is lighter: (′). In the example here, primary stress is placed on the first syllable; thus, the first accent mark is printed in a bolder typeface.

6. **Pronunciation:** (kun′ trē) The correct pronunciation of the main entry can be determined by examining the phonetic equivalent of the word, as shown in parentheses, and comparing it with the key to pronunciation found at the beginning of the dictionary.

7. **Part of Speech:** (*adj.*) The part of speech of the main entry is indicated by an italicized abbreviation following the pronunciation. A word having more than one part of speech is defined with each part of speech: **course** —*n.* onward movement or progress. —*v.* to race, run.

8. **Singular and Plural Forms:** (*pl.* **-tries**) If the main entry does not become plural by adding *s* or *es*, the notation *pl.* is shown followed by the plural form.

9. **Definitions:** (eight illustrated for *country*) The definition section of each main entry provides the meanings of that word. Since each dictionary uses its own entry pattern, check the one you are using. Some dictionaries give the most common definition first; others give the oldest definition first. (Through its explanatory notes, your dictionary will generally indicate the arrangement it uses.) Definitions are grouped by part of speech.

Although all dictionaries do not use the same pattern of notations, most dictionaries also contain the following:

10. **Word Etymology:** (<Old French *contree* <Medieval Latin *contrata* region lying opposite, etc.) The etymology indicates the origin of the main entry. When a word consists of a prefix, root word, and suffix, the etymology generally gives the origin of all three.

11. **Illustrative Sentences:** (*The pioneer women faced the hardships of the westward trek with courage.*) Illustrative sentences are printed in italics following a specific definition to show how the entry word is used with a particular meaning.

12. **Run-On Entry:** (—**cou ra′ geous ly,** *adv.*) A run-on entry is printed in small boldface type and lists undefined words. These words assume the meaning of the main entry plus the meaning of the suffix.

13. **Synonyms:** (**courage, bravery**) The synonym section of a main entry discusses words possessing meanings closely related to the main entry.

In addition, some dictionaries also include within the main entry antonyms, prefixes, suffixes, and foreign words and phrases.

Now open your dictionary and locate the word company. *For each dictionary part in the following list, fill in the blank with an appropriate example from your dictionary. Because dictionaries are different, answers will vary and are not provided. However, because you obtained the information directly from your dictionary, you can be assured of the accuracy of your answers.*

guide words _____   subentries _____

syllables _____   accent marks _____

pronunciation _____   part of speech _____

plural form _____   first definition _____

word etymology _____   synonyms _____

Now return to page 2 to check your answers to the pretest. How did you do? What have you learned?

Activity 1   *Identifying Syllables*

A syllable is any part of a word pronounced as a unit. The length of the word does not necessarily determine the number of syllables contained in a word. For example, the short word *idea* contains three syllables: **i de a**; and the longer word *demonstrate* also contains three syllables: **dem on strate**. As you say the words *idea* and *demonstrate*, you say three distinct sounds. Notice how your tongue glides from one syllable to the next.

In your dictionary, locate the word *administration*. Notice this word contains five syllables: **ad min is tra tion**.

Silent letters are included within the spelling of a syllable. For example, locate the word *debris*. Although the *s* is silent, this letter is included as part of the syllable: **de bris**. Occasionally we place extra syllables in some words. For example, how many syllables are in *athlete*? Sometimes we pronounce this word using three syllables, but the word contains only two: **ath lete**.

In addition, we sometimes ignore pronouncing certain syllables. For example, how many syllables are in *privilege*? If you said two, you would be wrong, but in good company. Check the dictionary, and you will find three syllables: **priv i lege**.

The following activity provides an opportunity for you to pronounce each of these fairly common words and determine the number of syllables.

Directions: *Pronounce each word and determine the number of syllables it contains. Then locate the word in your dictionary. On the blank line, write the word according to syllables.*

Word	Syllabication	Word	Syllabication
1. amateur	_____	11. period	_____
2. audience	_____	12. physical	_____
3. budget	_____	13. rhythm	_____
4. curriculum	_____	14. savory	_____
5. desperate	_____	15. sketchy	_____
6. funeral	_____	16. tantrum	_____
7. hospitable	_____	17. utopia	_____
8. leather	_____	18. violence	_____
9. majority	_____	19. width	_____
10. origin	_____	20. zirconium	_____

Activity 2   *Identifying Parts of Speech*

Immediately following each main entry's pronunciation, your dictionary indicates an abbreviation representing the word's part of speech. The eight parts of speech and their use in sentences are briefly described.

1. **Noun** (*n.*): A noun is a person, place, or thing, such as *Miss Stewart, Ricardo, Albuquerque,* and *computer.* Nouns may also be abstract, such as *reality, willingness,* and *ethics.*

2. **Pronoun** (*pron.*): A pronoun is a word referring to a person, place, or thing, and it is used in place of a noun; for example, *me, he, her, they, who,* and *those.*

3. **Verb** (*v.*): A verb is the most important word in a sentence because it shows the action of the noun. A verb may be either action or state of being (linking). Action verbs illustrate the action of the noun, such as *she wrote, he demonstrated,* and *the government spent.* A state-of-being verb shows no action and is usually a form of the verb *be*; for example, *are, is, were,* and *am.*

4. **Adjective** (*adj.*): An adjective modifies, describes, or gives meaning to a noun. Examples include *beautiful* surroundings, *tall* person, and *air-conditioned* office.

5. **Adverb** (*adv.*): An adverb modifies, describes, or gives meaning to a verb, an adjective, or another adverb. Adverbs usually answer the questions: How? When? Where? or To what extent? Examples include many *-ly* words, such as *frequently, slowly,* and *adequately,* as well as other words, such as *almost, very,* and *well.*

6. **Preposition** (*prep.*): A preposition is a word that shows the relationship of one word or set of words to another. Common prepositions include *of, for, to, among,* and *between.*

7. **Conjunction** (*conj.*): A conjunction joins words and word groups and includes words such as *and, or, but, however,* and *although.*

8. **Interjection** (*interj.*): An interjection is an isolated word expressing emotion. Examples include *Wow!* and *Ouch!* Interjections are typically followed by an exclamation point.

Your dictionary indicates the most common part of speech for each main entry, although additional parts of speech may be used for a given word.

Directions: *Using your dictionary, identify the commonly used part of speech for each of the following words and write the part of speech on the blank line following the word.*

Word	Part of Speech	Word	Part of Speech
1. an	_____	6. hurrah	_____
2. although	_____	7. needlessly	_____
3. by	_____	8. not	_____
4. compliance	_____	9. return	_____
5. helpful	_____	10. they	_____

WORD STUDIES

Activity 3   Identifying Words with Two Pronunciations

Most words have more than one definition, and hundreds of words can be used as more than one part of speech. Additionally, many words have more than one pronunciation.

Pronunciations sometimes vary according to geographical region. For example, if you are a southerner, you pronounce *pecan* differently than do westerners.

Two words spelled identically may be two different words stemming from different origins. They may even be different parts of speech. For example, if you enter a *contest* (noun), you may win a prize; but if you *contest* (verb) a clause in a contract, you may find yourself in court.

In addition, words are sometimes pronounced differently because the accent mark shifts in word usage. As you have questions, check your dictionary, because it lists all pronunciations followed by the parts of speech for each word.

Directions: *As you read each sentence, note the underlined word. On the blank line, write the syllabication of the underlined word followed by its part of speech as used in the sentence.*

1. Our network <u>affiliate</u> in Boston asked for a new promo advertising our fall lineup. _____

2. The president will <u>appropriate</u> funds to the projects indicated in his budget message. _____

3. The exemplary <u>conduct</u> of the parolee deserves consideration at her hearing. _____

4. To <u>convert</u> me to your ways, you will need to convince me. _____

5. Please <u>estimate</u> your needs before the committee meets Monday afternoon. _____

6. Because of <u>frequent</u> interruptions, we must relocate our meeting. _____

7. The new <u>initiate</u> spoke at the opening ceremonies. _____

8. The <u>insert</u> promptly fell on the ground as I retrieved the newspaper. _____

9. The <u>object</u> of our meeting is to ask for a raise. _____

10. If Edwin is to maintain job security, he must <u>produce</u> better work. _____

11. Our <u>progress</u> is beginning to create a new atmosphere. _____

12. Successful people quickly <u>rebound</u> when a financial setback occurs. _____

13. Asking for a <u>refund</u>, Elise detailed her justification. _____

14. Place the goods in three <u>separate</u> piles for the three charities. _____

15. Let's <u>survey</u> the membership to determine members' beliefs. _____

This review will help you to see what you have learned about using the dictionary.

Directions: *In your dictionary, locate the main entry listed in Column 1. On the blank line in Column 2, write the word according to syllables, placing the accent mark immediately after the stressed syllable. On the blank line in Column 3, write the part(s) of speech for the main entry. On the full blank line following each item, indicate any of the following that may be included in the word's dictionary entry: (1) plural form, (2) two pronunciations of the main entry, and (3) subentries.*

Main Entry	Syllabication	Part(s) of Speech
1. abstract		
2. banjo		
3. between		
4. cherub		
5. content		
6. demand		
7. duplicate		
8. ever		
9. index		
10. message		
11. obituary		
12. permit		
13. rebel		
14. somebody		
15. tight		

WORD STUDIES

Using the Thesaurus

Using a thesaurus will enhance your writing. Not only will your writing be more interesting, but it will come alive. A thesaurus is often the wake-up call for writing that serves as a sleeping pill.

Peter Mark Roget, who lived from 1779 to 1869, compiled the first thesaurus, which was appropriately titled *Roget's Thesaurus*. Today a number of Roget's thesauri are available in different formats and are published by different publishers. Because anyone can use the name *Roget*, be certain your thesaurus is published by a reputable publisher.

Each thesaurus uses its own style of presentation. Some use main entries in alphabetical order similar to dictionary entries. Others, including the *Roget's International Thesaurus*, 5th Edition, published by HarperCollins, use the style designed by Roget. In Roget's system, you must first know the word you wish to replace. Then you check the word in the index and pick the subentry closest to the meaning of the word you want. Follow the number of that word into the text of the book, and you will find an entire paragraph of synonyms.

Suppose, for example, you want to replace the word *sad* in an essay. If you check the index in the HarperCollins edition, you will find such classifications as *The Body and The Senses*, *Feelings*, *Living Things*, *The Mind and Ideas*, and 11 others. Because *sad* is a feeling, check Class 2, *Feelings*. Skimming down the column, you will find *112 Sadness*. Turning to *112*, on page 89, you will note *sadness* uses more than a page and a half to provide synonyms for several parts of speech. Because *sad* is an adjective, paragraphs 20–30 provide possible replacement words. Paragraphs 20, 21, and 22 are illustrated here.

ADJS **20 sad**, saddened; sadhearted, **sad of heart**; **heavyhearted**, heavy; oppressed, weighed upon, weighed or weighted down, bearing the woe of the world, burdened *or* laden with sorrow; sad-faced, long-faced; sad-eyed; sad-voiced

21 **unhappy**, **uncheerful**, uncheery, **cheerless**, **joyless**, **unjoyful**, unsmiling; mirthless, unmirthful, humorless, infestive; funny as a crutch <nonformal>; **grim**; **out of humor**, out of sorts, in bad humor *or* spirits; **sorry**, sorryish; discontented 108.5; wretched, miserable; pleasureless 96.20

22 **dejected**, **depressed**, **downhearted**, **down**, **downcast**, **cast down**, bowed down, subdued; **discouraged**, **disheartened**, **dispirited**, dashed; **low**, **feeling low**, low-spirited, **in low spirits**; **down in the mouth** <nonformal>, **in the doldrums**, **down in the dumps** *and* **in the dumps** *and* in the doleful dumps <all nonformal>, in the depths; **despondent**, desponding; **despairing** 125.12, weary of life, suicidal, world-weary; pessimistic 125.16; spiritless, heartless, **woebegone**; **drooping**, droopy, languishing, pining, haggard; hypochondriac *or* hypochondriacal

As a result of your search, you have a large number of alternatives for *sad*, including *saddened*, *unhappy*, *cheerless*, *grim*, *dejected*, *despondent*, and *woebegone*. Choose the word that best fits the meaning of the sentence.

For practice, use the index and replace several words of your choice or replace several of the following words: *blue*, *disappointed*, *big*, *disobey*, *speak*, *social class*, *money*, *basketball*, and *same*.

Using the Computerized Thesaurus

The increasing popularity of computerized word processors and their extended features have enabled thesaurus use on the computer to be easier and faster than using a printed copy. Although each word processor's thesaurus varies slightly, the principle of use remains the same.

The first step is to locate the function keys that access the thesaurus. Your word processing template or documentation will provide specific directions. After the correct keys have been depressed, your screen will display the thesaurus. At this point, one of two things could occur, depending on the location of the cursor on your screen:

1. If your cursor is positioned under a word, the thesaurus will provide a list of words that could be used to replace the word at the cursor.

2. If your cursor is not positioned under a word, the screen will ask you to input a word. Once that word has been keyed, the list of possible replacement words will appear on the screen.

For practice, access the thesaurus; then either input the word *ask* and position your cursor under this word, or input *ask* when the word prompt is displayed. Your screen will list the words that might replace *ask*. Typically a number or letter is shown next to most words. The letters or numbers indicate the synonyms of *ask* that are head words; that is, these words are also listed with a group of their own synonyms in the thesaurus. If a word does not have a number or letter, you cannot access additional words using that word.

For example, one synonym displayed for *ask* is *inquire*. If you press the indicated letter or number, you will be shown additional words that could be used as replacement words for *inquire*. These additional words also use numbers or letters to indicate other words. As you can see, you can go deeper and deeper into the thesaurus, searching for just the right word.

Your screen also contains other directions for using the thesaurus. You can, for example, replace the old word in your copy with the new word by following the directions. In addition, you can also clear columns, return to your document, and use additional indicated features.

Most thesaurus computer programs also provide antonyms to locate words meaning exactly the opposite of the replacement word.

Directions: *Key each of the following sentences; then replace the underlined words using your computerized thesaurus. Each of the sentences lacks color and creativity. Use your creativity to make them come alive.*

1. She is certainly a <u>petite</u> <u>young</u> girl.

2. The <u>old</u> man looks <u>youthful</u> for his age.

3. Please <u>acknowledge</u> receipt of this letter <u>soon</u>.

4. The actors <u>illustrate</u> their roles with a great amount of <u>flair</u>.

Activity 4   Using the Thesaurus

Directions: *You may use either a published thesaurus or a computerized thesaurus to complete this exercise. Column I lists a main entry followed by a part of speech. On the blank line to the right of the main entry, write a sentence using the word; then substitute a synonym of the main entry to enliven your sentence.*

1. adversity (*n.*) _____

2. careful (*adj.*) _____

3. frequent (*adj.*) _____

4. friend (*n.*) _____

5. go (*v.*) _____

6. great (*adj.*) _____

7. happy (*adj.*) _____

8. hope (*n.*) _____

9. hurt (*n.*) _____

10. liberal (*adj.*) _____

11. lost (*adj.*) _____

12. pleasantly (*adv.*) _____

13. real (*adj.*) _____

14. reject (*v.*) _____

15. see (*v.*) _____

16. skillful (*adj.*) _____

17. snub (*v.*) _____

18. tell (*v.*) _____

19. trip (*n.*) _____

20. very (*adv.*) _____

21. wish (*n.*) _____

22. wish (*v.*) _____

23. worker (*n.*) _____

24. wrong (*adv.*) _____

25. youthful (*adj.*) _____

Activity 5   *Using the Thesaurus for Synonyms and Antonyms*

Directions: *In your thesaurus, locate the main entry listed in Column 1, noting the indicated part of speech. On the blank line in Column 2, write a synonym of the main entry. On the blank line in Column 3, write an antonym for the main entry.*

Main Entry	Synonym	Antonym
1. appoint (*v.*)		
2. break (*n.*)		
3. cowardly (*adj.*)		
4. defend (*v.*)		
5. electrify (*v.*)		
6. feat (*n.*)		
7. gradual (*adj.*)		
8. hateful (*adj.*)		
9. important (*adj.*)		
10. juvenile (*n.*)		
11. lament (*v.*)		
12. malaise (*n.*)		
13. nomadic (*adj.*)		
14. obeisance (*n.*)		
15. patronize (*v.*)		
16. quantity (*n.*)		
17. resistance (*n.*)		
18. silly (*adj.*)		
19. thrifty (*adj.*)		
20. upright (*adj.*)		
21. vapid (*adj.*)		
22. wretched (*adj.*)		
23. yield (*v.*)		
24. zoom (*v.*)		

WORD STUDIES

Activity 6 Spelling Words Correctly—Set I

Directions: *Can you spell the 20 words in this exercise? Study the spelling of each word as well as its syllabication and definition. Then be prepared to write and define each word as directed by your instructor.*

1.	absence	ab sence	*n.* the condition of being away; lack of
2.	accommodate	ac com mo date	*v.* to have room for; to hold comfortably; to help out
3.	annihilate	an ni hi late	*v.* to destroy completely
4.	calendar	cal en dar	*n.* a table showing months, weeks, and days of the year
5.	colonel	colo nel	*n.* a commissioned officer in the U.S. armed services
6.	embarrass	em bar rass	*v.* to make uneasy, ashamed, and self-conscious
7.	extraordinary	ex traor di nar y	*adj.* remarkable; beyond the ordinary
8.	grateful	grate ful	*adj.* thankful; feeling kindly towards because of a favor done
9.	hiatus	hi a tus	*n.* an empty space; space from which something necessary for completeness is missing
10.	juvenile	ju ve nile	*n.* a young person; *adj.* youthful; immature
11.	liaison	li ai son	*n.* a connection between units; an illicit intimacy
12.	misspell	mis spell	*v.* to spell incorrectly
13.	ninety	nine ty	*n.* the number after 89; nine times ten
14.	pageant	pag eant	*n.* an elaborate spectacle featuring rich costuming
15.	privilege	priv i lege	*n.* a special right or advantage; *v.* to give a special right to
16.	psychology	psy chol o gy	*n.* the study of the mind; mental states and processes of people
17.	reservoir	res er voir	*n.* a place where water or something is collected and stored for use
18.	similar	sim i lar	*adj.* much the same; alike
19.	suspicion	sus pi cion	*n.* the state of mind of one who doubts another
20.	withhold	with hold	*v.* to refrain from giving; to keep back

Activity 7   Making Sense of Word Pairs—Set I

Directions: *Carefully study each pair of words. Associate the spelling with the word, the part of speech, and the definition. Note how the word is used in the illustrative sentence. Use each word as you write a sentence to be submitted to your instructor. Be prepared to write these words as directed by your instructor.*

1. accept   *v.*   to receive; to consent to take
   except   *v.*   to omit; to exclude; *prep.* but
   Everyone will readily *accept* the promotion plan *except* Lynn and David.

2. coarse   *adj.*   composed of large parts or particles; crude; vulgar
   course   *n.*   onward movement; direction taken; a unit of instruction; a place for games or races
   The *course* for the cross-country race includes an area of *coarse* ground.

3. device   *n.*   a mechanical invention used for a special purpose
   devise   *v.*   to invent; to plan
   Using my *device* and your thought process, you can *devise* a concrete plan of action.

4. every one   *pron.*   every person, with *one* stressed
   everyone   *pron.*   everybody, with *every* stressed
   This year our football team won *every one* of its games because *everyone* came together as a team.

5. illegible   *adj.*   very difficult or impossible to read
   ineligible   *adj.*   not qualified; unfit
   All *illegible* entries will be ruled *ineligible,* then disqualified from the contest.

6. its   *adj.*   possessive form of *it*; belonging to it
   it's   *pron. + v.*   contraction of *it is* and *it has*
   The book and *its* summary are on the desk; *it's* time to begin your report.

7. moral   *adj.*   good in character and conduct; virtuous; *n.* lesson drawn from a story or message
   morale   *n.*   the mental condition or attitude of a person or group; enthusiasm
   The *moral* of her parable is that if an employer meets employees' needs, then company *morale* will be improved.

8. personal   *adj.*   private; pertaining to an individual; done by oneself
   personnel   *n.*   the people employed in a business, work, or service
   The *personnel* at Scrooge Industries are not allowed to make *personal* calls.

9. set   *v.*   to place; to put in place; to cause to be arranged; *n.* group; outfit
   sit   *v.*   to rest on the lower part of the body; to hold a session; to be a member of a council; to pose
   Please *sit* down, *set* your bags on the table, and rest a few minutes.

10. stationary   *adj.*   fixed; standing still; not changing
    stationery   *n.*   writing materials, such as paper and envelopes
    Envelopes can be purchased at the *stationery* shop located behind the *stationary* bus sign across the street.

Activity 8 *Business-Related Terminology—Set 1*

The business-related terminology exercises contained in this book focus on terms common in everyday business usage.

Directions: *Learn the following 15 words and their meanings; then be prepared to write and define them as directed by your instructor.*

1. **automated teller machine (ATM)** *n.* an unattended banking station that pays cash from, or receives deposits into, an individual's account upon use of a bank-issued card

2. **beneficiary** *n.* the person named in an insurance policy entitled to receive the policy's proceeds upon the death of the insured

3. **bipartisan** *adj.* supported or represented by the two major political parties

4. **certificate of deposit (CD)** *n.* a fixed-time-period savings that pays greater interest than regular savings

5. **collateral** *n.* an asset of marketable property a borrower pledges as security for a loan

6. **deficit** *n.* a shortage; an amount spent for which cash is not available to cover

7. **electronic funds transfer (EFT)** *n.* the use of computers and electronic means to transfer money from one account to another or from one party to another

8. **equal opportunity employer (EOE)** *n.* an employer who hires qualified employees without regard to age, gender, race, or religion

9. **fringe benefit** *n.* a benefit given to an employee in addition to wages, such as health insurance, paid vacations, etc.

10. **net income** *n.* the amount of income received after taxes and other deductions have been subtracted

11. **premium** *n.* the rate per unit of insurance coverage multiplied by the number of insurance units purchased, consisting of the amount the insured pays each period

12. **recession** *n.* a period of temporary business reduction marked by layoffs from work in some areas

13. **remuneration** *n.* the payment received for services rendered

14. **subpoena** *n.* an official document ordering a person to appear in court

15. **time deposits** *n.* interest-bearing accounts with commercial banks that carry specified maturity dates and are subject to penalty for early withdrawal

Activity 9   Computer-Related Terminology—Set 1

Because we live in the computer age, new words related to the computer are coined and old words are given new definitions. This section presents a set of computer-related terms in each part. This first set of words relates to general computer usage.

Directions: *Learn the following 15 words and their meanings; then be prepared to write and define them as directed by your instructor.*

1. **architecture**   *n.*   the physical design of computer hardware or of a particular output

2. **artificial intelligence**   *n.*   computer applications resembling human intelligence; a field concerned with ways computers can simulate human intelligence

3. **bar code**   *n.*   a product code read by an automated reader directly into the computer; the computer, in turn, responds with certain information, such as the product price

4. **bug**   *n.*   an error in a software program

5. **compact disk (CD)**   *n.*   a small, round optical disk used for storing information to be read by the computer

6. **computer-assisted instruction (CAI)**   *n.*   self-paced learnings accomplished by a student using a computer

7. **desktop publishing**   *n.*   software that prints text and graphics with a professional appearance

8. **documentation**   *n.*   printed instructions detailing the operation of a program or system

9. **electronic mail**   *n.*   the electronic transmission of memos and documents through a communications network

10. **laptop**   *adj., n.*   a small, powerful computer capable of being carried

11. **network**   *n.*   a group of computers joined together for user communications and program sharing

12. **peripheral**   *n.*   any hardware device, such as a printer, connected to a computer

13. **printout**   *n.*   the hard copy produced by a printing, symbolizing printer output

14. **screen dump**   *n.*   printing to a printer the contents of the screen

15. **user-friendly**   *adj.*   implies an easy-to-understand dialogue between the user and the computer program

The Dictionary and Thesaurus

I. Using the Dictionary. **Directions:** *Identify each circled part of the dictionary entries in the following illustration. Locate the identified part in the list that follows the illustration, and write the corresponding number on the appropriate blank.*

E e

E[1] or e (ē), *n., pl.* E's or e's. the fifth letter of the English alphabet.
E[2] (ē), n., pl. E's, the third tone of the musical scale of C major.
e-, prefix. form of ex-[1] before consonants except c, f, p, q, s, t, as in evaporate, emerge.
E, **1** East or east. **2** Eastern or eastern. **3** einsteinium. **4** English.
ea., each.
each (ēch), adj. being one (of two or more persons, things, etc.) considered separately

6 a careful or favorable hearing; attention.
be all ears, INFORMAL, listen eagerly.
believe one's ears, credit what one hears.
play by ear, a play (a piece of music or a musical instrument) without using written music. **b** handle (a matter) without adequate

me di um (mē′dē əm), *adj., n., pl.* **-di ums** or (also for 2, 3, 4) **-di a. —***adj.* having a middle position, quality, or condition; moderate: *of medium height.* —*n.* **1** something that is in the middle in nature or degree; neither one extreme nor the other; middle condition. **2** substance or agent through which anything acts; a means: *Television and radio are media of communication. Money is a medium of exchange in trading.* **3** substance in which something can live; environment: *Water is the natural medium of fish.* **4** a nutritive substance in or upon which microorganisms are grown for study. **5** liquid with which paints are mixed. **6** person through whom messages from the spirits of the dead are supposedly sent to the living. [< Latin, neuter of *medius* middle]
medium frequency, (in electronics) a frequency ranging from 300 to 3000 kilocycles per second.

shark
shark[2] (shärk), *n.* **1** a dishonest person who preys on others. **2** SLANG. person unusually good at something; expert: *a shark at poker.* —*v.i.* act or live by preying on others; live by trickery. [probably < German *Schurke* scoundrel]
shark skin (shärk′skin′), *n.* **1** fabric made from fine threads of wool, rayon, or cotton, used in suits. **2** skin of a shark. **3** leather made from the skin of a shark.
sharp (shärp), *adj.* **1** having a thin cutting edge or a fine point: *a sharp knife, a pencil with a sharp point.* **2** having or coming to a point; not rounded: *a sharp nose, a sharp corner on a box.* **3** with a sudden change of direction: *a sharp turn in the road.* **4** very cold: *sharp weather.* **5** severe; biting: *sharp*

_____ accent mark	_____ pronunciation
_____ definition	_____ plural form
_____ guide word	_____ subentry
_____ main entry	_____ syllable
_____ part of speech	_____ compound-word entry

II. Using the Thesaurus. **Directions:** *Each sentence or sentence fragment contains one or two underlined words. Use your thesaurus and replace each underlined word with a word that fits the meaning of the sentence. To complete the meaning, you may also use a derivative of any words not underlined. Write the words on the lines at the right.*

1. the <u>big</u> city _____

2. I <u>feel</u> ill. _____

3. I will <u>deal with</u> you later. _____

4. a <u>pretty</u> young lady _____

5. a <u>handsome</u> gentleman _____

6. a <u>rich miser</u> _____

7. to <u>sit</u> down _____

8. a <u>frequently</u> used word _____

9. a <u>complete fool</u> _____

10. a <u>loathsome oaf</u> _____

Review   *Special Word Lists*

Directions: *On the blank in each sentence, write the business-related or computer-related term described by the sentence. Then edit each sentence by drawing a line through all misspelled and misused words and writing the correct spelling directly above or directly below the incorrectly spelled or used word.*

1. A hardware devise connected to the computer that allows the computer to acommodate its use is called a _____ .

2. An unattended banking station that allows any one the priviledge of withdrawing cash using the proper card is a(n) _____ .

3. A _____ computer is similiar to a personnel computer accept it is smaller and capable of being carried.

4. The calender is used to determine when the _____ should be paid to keep insurance in force.

5. An adult or a juvinile can set down at a computer and have no problems using software that is _____ .

6. A _____ bill will be excepted by both political parties.

7. _____ may be used in any coarse with the absense of a regular textbook.

8. People who have a _____ in their accounts may be embarassed, particularly if they are under suspision of overspending.

9. _____ , including any mispelled words, is written instructions that provide an effective liason between the software and the user.

10. Money is transferred via computer using _____ , negating a problem with ineligible writing that possibly could anihilate a bank account.

11. No stationary is used with mail sent through the computer using a process known as _____ .

12. Extras, called _____ , help improve employee moral by giving employees values they are usually greatful to receive.

13. A _____ in the software can cause a haitus and can withold vital information.

14. A fixed-time-period, such as ninty days, savings that often pays extrordinary interest is a _____ .

WORD STUDIES

WORKING
WITH
WORDS

Working with Words		20
Activity 10	**The Hyphen/Compound Words**	21
Activity 11	**Words with the Sound of** *seed*	22
Activity 12	**Words with Silent** *gh*/**Words with** *ph* **Sounding like** *f*	23
Activity 13	**Words Ending in** *e* **and** *ie*	24
Activity 14	**Words Ending in** *y*	25
	Working with Words: Review	26
Activity 15	**Words Containing** *ei* **and** *ie*—**Set 1**	27
Activity 16	**Words Containing** *ei* **and** *ie*—**Set 2**	28
Activity 17	**Malapropisms**	29
Activity 18	**Words Containing Double Letters**	30
Activity 19	**Spelling Words Correctly—Set 2**	31
Activity 20	**Making Sense of Word Pairs—Set 2**	32
Activity 21	**Business-Related Terminology—Set 2**	33
Activity 22	**Computer-Related Terminology—Set 2**	34
	Working with Words: Review	35
	Special Word Lists: Review	36

Part

2

■ Working with Words

The activities in this part have been deliberately selected to enable you to review a number of words and word groups that even the best spellers sometimes confuse in usage. These words will cause you no difficulty, however, if you master the guidelines for

- ■ compound words
- ■ the correct spelling of words with the sound of *seed*
- ■ words with silent *gh*
- ■ words containing *ph* that sounds like *f*
- ■ words ending in *y*, *e*, and *ie*
- ■ words containing *ie* and *ei*

To see how you relate to these word challenges, complete the following pretest.

Directions: *The first column lists a short phrase containing one or more misspelled or misused words. On the blank line at the right, write the correct spelling of all misspelled words in the first column.*

1. prosede thru the barreir _____

2. the semi-annual procedings _____

3. an autograf exposeure _____

4. dieing for triumf _____

5. the donkeies lazyness _____

6. a foriegn shiek _____

7. irational, tring behavior _____

8. formmer namless employer _____

9. hygeine product from farmacy _____

10. non-member familys _____

Now check your answers: (1) proceed through, barrier; (2) semiannual proceedings; (3) autograph exposure; (4) dying, triumph; (5) donkey's laziness; (6) foreign sheik; (7) irrational, trying; (8) former nameless; (9) hygiene, pharmacy; (10) nonmember families.

Mark your success. Consider returning to this page after you have completed the exercises in this part and completing the pretest once more to see your improvement.

Activity 10   The Hyphen/Compound Words

Compound words can be grouped in three categories: the open compound, the solid compound, and the hyphenated compound. An **open compound** is a combination of two or more words so closely associated they constitute a single concept, but they are spelled as separate words without a hyphen. Examples include *savings account*, *postal service*, and *peanut butter*. A **solid compound** is a combination of two or more words spelled as one word without a hyphen, such as *earthquake*, *butterfly*, and *database*. A **hyphenated compound** is a combination of two or more words or affixes joined by a hyphen, such as *self-reliance*, *pro-American*, and *built-in*.

The following guidelines indicate when a hyphen is appropriately placed in a compound.

1. Use a hyphen in spelling compound numbers from twenty-one to ninety-nine and with fractions used as adjectives, but not as nouns: *one-half* share, *one half* of the pie.

2. Use a hyphen to avoid ambiguity: *recover* a stolen chair, *re-cover* a chair in need of upholstery.

3. Use a hyphen in compounds containing a prepositional phrase unless the dictionary indicates the preferred spelling is without the hyphen: *brother-in-law*, *mother-of-pearl*, *editor in chief*, *attorney at law*.

4. Use a hyphen after any prefix preceding a proper noun or adjective: *pre-Easter* sale, *post-Christmas* specials.

5. Use a hyphen with all *self* words except *selfish* and *selfless* and their derivatives, such as *selfishly* and *selflessly*. Examples of *self* words with hyphens include *self-confidence*, *self-addressed*, and *self-evaluation*.

6. Use a hyphen with a compound adjective or an adjective when a noun follows, such as *air-conditioning* unit and *second-class* citizen.

Hyphens need not be used with other prefixes, such as *non* and *semi*, unless they adhere to one of the above guidelines or unless the word is hyphenated in the dictionary.

Directions: *On the blank lines at the right, correctly rewrite the words. Use your dictionary and the rules you just learned to write each word as an open compound, a solid compound, or a hyphenated compound.*

1. by stander _____

2. county seat _____

3. double take _____

4. go between _____

5. hand out (n.) _____

6. land slide _____

7. notary public _____

8. old fashioned (adj.) _____

9. patrol wagon _____

10. self improvement _____

11. semi annual _____

12. write in _____

Activity 11   *Words with the Sound of* seed

Because of their identical pronunciations, words containing the sound of *seed* often cause confusion in writing and spelling. Remembering three guidelines will enable you to spell all *seed* words correctly.

1. **sede:** Only one word—*supersede*—and its derivatives use this spelling. Its derivatives include *superseding* and *superseded.*

2. **ceed:** Only three words—*exceed, proceed,* and *succeed*—and their derivatives use this spelling. Derivatives of these words include *exceeding, proceeds,* and *succeeded.* A mnemonic sentence, such as "A business *succeeds* when its *proceeds exceed* expenses," can help you remember these words.

3. **cede:** All other words containing the sound of *seed* use the spelling *cede.* These words include *intercede, precede, accede,* and their modifications, such as *procedure* and *interceding.*

Directions: *On the blank line following each prefix, write* sede, ceed, *or* cede *to spell the word correctly in the sentence. In some derivatives, you may need to alter the spelling slightly to spell the word correctly.*

1. Let's pro_____ to the next item on the agenda.

2. Super_____ing all previous instructions, use this list for guidance.

3. The owner of Natchez Enterprises is ex_____ingly rich.

4. The pro_____ings of the conference have been recorded and are available for purchase.

5. If you ac_____ to my request, you'll make me happy.

6. The waters began to re_____ as the sun warmed the earth.

7. Using the right pro_____ure, you'll do well on your skills test.

8. My orders super_____ those you received.

9. If you are to suc_____ with your objective, you must plan ahead.

10. The incumbent mayor decided to con_____ the election when the results became apparent.

11. Please inter_____ with Mr. Francis for me; I'm getting nowhere.

12. The flag bearers should pre_____ the grand marshall in the parade.

13. The ante_____nt of any pronoun must be an obvious noun.

14. If you ex_____ the speed limit, you may have to pay a fine.

15. The pre_____ing message was paid for by the Mary Owens for Mayor committee.

Activity 12 Words with Silent gh/Words with ph *Sounding like* f

A **digraph** is two consecutive letters that together create a single sound. Most digraphs cause little confusion, such as *wh* in *what*, *th* in *that*, and *ch* in *church*. Some potential problems occur, however, when a digraph produces a sound different from either of its individual letters or when a digraph produces no sound at all. Two such digraphs are *gh* and *ph*.

The digraph *gh* is frequently silent, as in *nigh* and *slight*. The digraph *gh* generally appears at the end of a word, as in *bough* and *though*; or it may be followed by the letter *t*, as in *bought* and *thought*. One common exception is *neighbor*.

The digraph *ph* generally takes the sound of *f*, as in *pharmacy*, *alphabet*, and *photograph*. The primary exceptions occur when two shorter words are joined together, with the first word ending in *p* and the second word beginning with *h*, as in *haphazard* and *loophole*.

Directions: *On the blank line at the right, correctly spell all misspelled words in the sentence.*

1. Christofer Columbus believed the sfere was round; hindsit proved him rit.

   _____

2. Althou Marcus appeared delited, he had many fobias and was fritened by frequent nitmares.

   _____

3. Our team had a rouf game, but we were toufer and triumfed to win the trofy.

   _____

4. The pamflet describes the side effects of the pills prescribed by my fiscian, Dr. Jones, and purchased at the farmacy. _____

5. My neibor is very nearsited, having been tested by an ofthalmologist.

   _____

6. *Slauter on Tenth Avenue* has been choreografed as a musical fantasy on asfalt.

   _____

7. We had a catastrofe on our hiway; the semafore stopped working at twilite, creating a fatal accident.

   _____

8. Her biografy indicated she fout to save animals, especially dolfins and elefants.

   _____

9. The atmosfere for nitlife at the hibrow club comes to naut when midnite approaches.

   _____

10. Graceland, in Memfis, shows Elvis at the heit of his career, with his trofies, thorobreds, and autografed memorabilia. _____

11. I emfasize how emfatic I am about your shunning fony riteous people during your sofomore year.

   _____

12. Please transcribe the material from the dictafone and send a fotocopy to my weit trainer in Ralei, North Carolina. _____

Activity 13   *Words Ending in* e *and* ie

When words end with an *e*, this final *e* is usually silent. Although the words themselves create no problems, sometimes difficulties occur when suffixes are added. Use the following guidelines to add suffixes to such words:

Rule 1. Words Ending in Silent *e*

When words end in silent *e* and are preceded by a consonant, retain the *e* when adding a suffix beginning with a consonant: improv*e* + *ment* = improve*ment*.

When words end in silent *e* and are preceded by a consonant, drop the *e* when adding a suffix beginning with a vowel: revok*e* + *able* = revok*able*.

When words end in a silent *e* and are preceded by the vowel *o*, retain the final *e* when adding the suffix -*ing*: ho*e* + *ing* = ho*eing*. When words end in a silent *e* and are preceded by a vowel other than *o*, generally drop the *e* when adding the suffix: argu*e* + *ing* = argu*ing*.

When words end in *ce* with the *c* sounding like *s* or *z*, and when words end in *ge* with the *g* sounding like *j*, generally retain the final *e*: enforc*e* + *able* = enforc*eable*, chang*e* + *able* = chang*eable*.

An exception is charg*e* + *ing* = charg*ing*. This exception will occur most often with the suffixes -*ed* and -*ing*. In addition, several words may be spelled with or without the *e*. In such instances, the first preference is to omit the *e*: *abridgment, acknowledgment, judgment.*

Rule 2. Words Ending in *ie*

When words end in *ie*, drop the *e* and change the *i* to *y* when adding the suffix -*ing*. This rule prevents two *i*'s from coming together: vi*e* + *ing* = v*ying*.

Directions: *Combine the root word and the suffix for each of the following items, and write the new word on the blank line.*

1. arise + ing _____
2. blame + less _____
3. change + able _____
4. charge + able _____
5. commence + ment _____
6. continue + ing _____
7. delete + ion _____
8. die + ing _____
9. expose + ure _____
10. grace + ful _____

11. guide + ance _____
12. lie + ing _____
13. provoke + ing _____
14. refuse + al _____
15. rescue + er _____
16. score + less _____
17. televise + ion _____
18. tie + ing _____
19. toe + ing _____
20. woe + ful _____

Activity 14   Words Ending in y

Rules 3 and 4 provide guidelines for adding a suffix to a root word ending in *y*.

Rule 3. Words Ending in *y* Preceded by a Consonant

When words end in *y* and are preceded by a consonant, generally change the *y* to *i* and add the suffix: harmo<u>ny</u> + <u>ous</u> = harmon<u>ious</u>.

When the suffix begins with *i*, the *y* is generally retained: lob<u>by</u> + <u>ing</u> = lobb<u>ying</u>.

When the suffix *s* is added to the root word and the *y* is changed to *i*, the suffix is generally spelled *-ies*: utili<u>ty</u> + <u>s</u> = utilit<u>ies</u>.

One-syllable words ending in *y* do not consistently apply Rule 3: p<u>ry</u> + <u>ed</u> = pr<u>ied</u>, d<u>ry</u> + <u>ly</u> = dry<u>ly</u>.

Several exceptions to Rule 3 also exist, including *beauteous, charitable*, and *shyness*. Furthermore, a word ending in *y* consisting of two shorter words does not necessarily change the *y* to *i*, such as in *everything* and *myself*.

Rule 4. Words Ending in *y* Preceded by a Vowel

When words end in *y* and are preceded by a vowel, the *y* is retained when the suffix is added: attorn<u>ey</u> + <u>s</u> = attorne<u>ys</u>, destr<u>oy</u> + <u>ing</u> = destro<u>ying</u>.

Irregular verbs—verbs that do not form the past tense by adding *d* or *ed*—do not follow Rule 4: s<u>ay</u> + <u>ed</u> = s<u>aid</u>, l<u>ay</u> + <u>ed</u> = l<u>aid</u>.

Directions: *The following short phrases contain a root word ending in y followed by a suffix enclosed in parentheses. On the blank line, add the suffix to the root and write the correctly spelled word.*

1. the music's amplify(cation) _____

2. the army(s) of Allied nations _____

3. a confidence betray(ed) _____

4. several body(s) of evidence _____

5. look folks, no cavity(s) _____

6. a charity(able) contribution _____

7. you caught me cry(ing) _____

8. deploy(ing) a strategy _____

9. total enjoy(ment) _____

10. two family(s) meet _____

11. get out your fry(er) _____

12. happy(ness) abounds _____

13. favorite holiday(s) _____

14. someone lucky(er) than I _____

15. money(s) from three countries _____

16. were you pay(d) _____

17. they say(d) _____

18. certain amount of shy(ness) _____

19. supply(ing) the troops _____

20. we've been try(ing) _____

This review allows you to check your progress by applying the guidelines for compound words, words with the sound of *seed*, words with the silent *gh*, words with the *ph* sounding like *f*, words ending in *e* and *ie*, and words ending in *y*.

Directions: *Edit the following essay. Write the correct spelling of all misspelled or misused words on the blank line following each paragraph.*

Altho he dyed in 1977, Elvis Presley remains the riteful "King of Rock." Even today no one has superceded his fame.

_____

His biografy begins in 1935 in Tupelo, Mississippi, where Elvis lived in deploreable poverty until he began performing in 1953. Three years later, Elvis exceded all expectations as he joined the ranks of national celebritys.

_____

Elvis became fameous in 1956 with his number 1 hit "Heartbreak Hotel." He then succeded as an overnite success with additional hits, including "All Shook Up," "Don't Be Cruel," "Hound Dog," "Jailhouse Rock," and the lovly ballad, "Love Me Tender," which made young ladys swoon.

_____

His first appearance on the *Ed Sullivan Show* was in 1956, when cameras displaed his body only from the waist up. Many people were annoied that Ed wouldn't intersede to stop some one gyrateing his hips.

_____

Music critics were not lieing when they sayed he was the mastermind of rock music, preceeding all future rock artists.

_____

Althou records were his emfasis, he starred in 33 motion pictures, beginning in 1956 with *Love Me Tender*.

_____

Selfconscious of his image, Elvis proved to be proAmerican as he served in the military for the Allied countrys during the Korean conflict.

_____

After overdoseing on drugs in August 1977, Elvis passed away. He is buryed at Graceland, outside Memfis, Tennessee.

_____

Today Graceland is open to the public for payed tours. Tickets for an enjoiable tour can be purchased across the street from Graceland. From there, shuttle vans take people to the mansion. The tour includes five rooms of the mansion, the spacious grounds, and exhibits featureing his fameous jumpsuits, guitars, and grafic fotos. While you are waiting for your tour, purchases can be made for several sites, includeing his two air planes. In addition, you can buy tapes and CDs from record stores, post-cards from gift shops, and lunch from Heartbreak Cafe.

_____

For all anniversarys of his death, thousands of fans flock to Graceland for a candlelit vigil. Thou the King is gone, memorys of him linger.

_____

Activity 15   Words Containing ei and ie—Set 1

The most confusing spelling problem for many is knowing when to use *ei* or *ie* when this combination appears in a word. For example, is the word *foreign* or *foriegn* correct? *sheik* or *shiek*? *weird* or *wierd*? Although exceptions still occur, the following rule presents usage guidelines.

Rule 5. The *ei* and *ie* Sequences

When *e* and *i* occur together in a word, the *i* generally precedes the *e* except in the following circumstances:

■   when the sound of long *e* follows *c*: con<u>cei</u>ve, de<u>cei</u>t

■   when the two vowels are pronounced as long *a*: n<u>ei</u>ghbor, sl<u>ei</u>gh

■   when the two vowels are pronounced as long *i*: sl<u>ei</u>ght, Fahrenh<u>ei</u>t

■   when the two vowels are pronounced as short *i* following *f*: forf<u>ei</u>t, caff<u>ei</u>ne

■   when the word begins with these two letters, the combination is always *ei*: <u>ei</u>ght, <u>ei</u>ther

Several common exceptions to this rule are *foreign*, *heifer*, *heir*, *leisure*, *neither*, *protein*, *seize*, *sovereign*, *their*, and *weird*.

Directions: *The first column contains a word spelled with both the* ei *and* ie *sequences. On the blank line to the right of each word, write the correct spelling of the word.*

1. acheive/achieve _____

2. atheist/athiest _____

3. ceiling/cieling _____

4. chandeleir/chandelier _____

5. feisty/fiesty _____

6. feiry/fiery _____

7. freight/frieght _____

8. greif/grief _____

9. heighten/hieghten _____

10. leisure/liesure _____

11. leiutenant/lieutenant _____

12. obedeince/obedience _____

13. perceive/percieve _____

14. peir/pier _____

15. receipt/reciept _____

16. releive/relieve _____

17. seige/siege _____

18. stein/stien _____

19. veil/viel _____

20. weight/wieght _____

Activity 16   Words Containing *ei* and *ie*—Set 2

Directions: *Edit each of the following sentences. For each* ei *and* ie *word that is spelled incorrectly, write the correct spelling on the blank line to the right of each sentence.*

1. Before your interveiw, reveiw your qualifications, wieghing each by importance.

   _____
   _____

2. "Let's go on a sliegh ride," she called impateintly.

   _____

3. His breifcase contained not only his books but also cans of his decaffienated beverage.

   _____
   _____

4. Put on your coat to sheild you from the cold; it's 32 degrees Fahrenhiet outside.

   _____
   _____

5. For the hienous crime, the theif was given 30 years in the state prison.

   _____
   _____

6. That chiffonneir has been in my family for 80 years; it's practically a hierloom.

   _____
   _____

7. The ticket was on her windsheild as she exited the oreintation; it was her forteith parking ticket.

   _____
   _____

8. For lunch, you can have weiners or refreid beans.

   _____

9. The soveriegn began a riegn of terror after siezing control of the military.

   _____
   _____

10. A fiesty young lady, Jennifer is both resileint and mischeivous.

    _____

11. The drunken soldeir claimed sobreity but was unable to walk a straight line.

    _____
    _____

12. To avoid being recognized, the fraulien placed a viel over her face.

    _____
    _____

13. Qualifying for the preisthood, Brother Mondale said he diefied his maker; he was no athiest.

    _____
    _____

14. Get a vareity of protien in your deit and pay attention to your hygeine.

    _____
    _____

15. We will be forced to forfiet our afternoon seista unless you can concieve a plan of action.

    _____
    _____

Activity 17　Malapropisms

Richard Sheridan's classic play *The Rivals*, first performed in 1775, contained a comic character named Mrs. Malaprop, who slaughtered the English language by ridiculously misusing words. Her name stuck, and today we use the term *malapropism* for words misused to the point of being ridiculous.

For example, Mrs. Malaprop discussed geographical areas as being *contagious countries* instead of *contiguous countries*. Instead of calling a brilliant person *intellectual*, she called him or her *ineffectual*. In addition, Mrs. Malaprop referred to:

- having great *affluence*, instead of *influence*
- receiving a *preposition*, instead of *proposition*
- having *allusions* of grandeur, instead of *delusions*
- thinking of a *supercilious* thing, instead of *superficial*

Even today, we have our own malapropisms. For example, have you heard any of the following:

- *taken for granite*, instead of *taken for granted* (Who wants to be taken for a rock?)
- *very close veins* instead of *varicose veins* (Don't we all have them?)
- *unthawed* instead of *thawed* (Technically, *unthawed* means "frozen." Are you in the habit of eating food that's frozen?)

Directions: *Read each sentence and circle the word at the right that belongs in the blank space.*

1. Doreen correctly defined a _____ as a part of speech that shows relationship to the noun or pronoun.　　preposition/proposition

2. What a sales force! Kent could _____ an igloo resident into buying a refrigerator.　　affluence/influence

3. Demonstrating professional _____, Dr. Ruth Stanger stopped and helped the accident victim.　　benevolence/malevolence

4. Seeking counseling, Ursula felt her husband had begun taking her for _____.　　granite/granted

5. At the Four Corners region, Utah, Arizona, New Mexico, and Colorado are _____ to each other.　　contagious/contiguous

6. My mother's _____ has often prevented potential grief for members of our family.　　intuition/tuition

7. Sorry to _____, but I am leaving and must give you these messages.　　intercept/interrupt

8. During his testimony before the grand jury, Alvin made an _____ to his involvement in the incident.　　allusion/illusion

9. Since changing to a capitalistic society, the nation is becoming _____.　　autonomous/monotonous

10. If you eat a well-balanced diet in _____ with getting sufficient exercise, you'll feel better.　　conjunction/injunction

Activity 18   Words Containing Double Letters

The following five points provide guidelines for doubling letters in words:

1. **Double Letters Formed by Addition of a Suffix.** When a suffix beginning with a vowel is joined to

   ■ a one-syllable word ending in a consonant preceded by a vowel or

   ■ a word of more than one syllable ending in a consonant preceded by a vowel with no change in accent,

   ■ the final letter of the root word is doubled: ship + ed = shipped, remit + ing = remitting.

2. **Double Letters Formed by Addition of a Prefix.** When a root word is joined to a prefix and the last letter of the prefix is the same as the first letter of the root word, both letters are generally retained: mis + spell = misspell, ir + replaceable = irreplaceable.

3. **Double Letters Formed by a Compound Word.** When two short words are joined to form a compound word, the original spelling of both words is generally retained: book + keeper = bookkeeper, with + hold = withhold.

4. **Double Letters Formed by Association.** Although not generally related in meaning, some words with double letters can be associated with others that may or may not have double letters because they sound or are spelled in a similar manner. Such words should be memorized: *harass* and *embarrass*, *accommodate* and *recommend*.

5. **Double Letters Formed in Word Origin.** Many words contain double letters stemming from their origin: *chauffeur, necessary, occasion, omission*.

Directions: *Each sentence contains at least one misspelled word because of a double letter. On the blank line to the right of each sentence, correctly spell each misspelled word.*

1. The personel department will form a comittee to evaluate our hiring policies.   _____   _____

2. Having recuring nightmares, Kyle sought profesional asistance.   _____   _____

3. If apropriate in your adress, please mention the necesity of avoiding diservice when working with the public.   _____   _____

4. The bookeeper indicated witholding taxes are aproximately 20 percent for your salary bracket.   _____   _____

5. Comission on all sales acounts will be paid imediately.   _____   _____

6. He admited he behaved irationaly before his sucessful therapy.   _____   _____

7. She reccomended her roomate be considered for the openning in marketting.   _____   _____

8. All corespondence should be sent to the atention of Mr. Davis in Data Proccessing efective June 1.   _____   _____

Activity 19   Spelling Words Correctly—Set 2

Directions: *The 20 words in this exercise may be familiar to you. Study the spelling of each word as well as its syllabication and definition. Then be prepared to write and define each word as directed by your instructor.*

1.	acquittal	ac quit tal	*n.*	discharge; a being set free because of a not-guilty verdict
2.	canceled	can celed	*v.*	to cross out, delete; to put an end to
3.	chauffeur	chauf feur	*n.*	a person who drives an automobile for others; *v.* to drive another
4.	dilemma	di lem ma	*n.*	a situation requiring a choice between two unpleasant alternatives
5.	etiquette	et i quette	*n.*	customary rules for behavior in society
6.	grammar	gram mar	*n.*	the study of words and their forms and uses in a language
7.	harass	har ass	*v.*	to trouble by repeated attacks; to disturb
8.	hemorrhage	hem or rhage	*n.*	a heavy discharge of blood; *v.* to lose much blood
9.	medieval	me di e val	*adj.*	having to do with the Middle Ages
10.	occasion	oc ca sion	*n.*	a particular time; special event; opportunity
11.	omission	o mis sion	*n.*	something left out
12.	parallel	par al lel	*adj.*	lying or extending alongside of one another; *v.* to be at the same distance from throughout the length
13.	penicillin	pen i cil lin	*n.*	an antibiotic made from molds to treat disease
14.	programmed	pro grammed	*v.*	any event, series, or list prepared to be used
15.	questionnaire	ques tion naire	*n.*	a written set of questions used to gather information
16.	recommend	rec om mend	*v.*	to speak in favor of; to advise
17.	renaissance	ren ais sance	*n.*	new birth; revival
18.	sheriff	sher iff	*n.*	the chief law-enforcing officer in a county
19.	sovereign	sov er eign	*n.*	the supreme ruler of a country; monarch; *adj.* having supreme rank or authority
20.	tariff	tar iff	*n.*	a list of duties or taxes a government charges on imports or exports

Activity 20   Making Sense of Word Pairs—Set 2

Directions: *Carefully study each pair of words. Associate the spelling with the word, the part of speech, and the definition. Note how the word is used in the illustrative sentence. Use each word as you write a sentence to be submitted to your instructor. Be prepared to write these words as directed by your instructor.*

1. accede — *v.* to give in; to consent; to become a party to
   exceed — *v.* to be more or greater than; to go beyond

   Please *accede* to the officer's request to never *exceed* the speed limit.

2. biannual — *adj.* occurring twice a year
   biennial — *adj.* occurring every two years; *n.* plant that lives for two years

   She has slightly more than a year left on her *biennial* appointment as she edits her second *biannual* publication due out June 15.

3. boom — *n.* a long, deep, hollow sound; a sudden increase in business; *v.* to make a rumbling noise
   boon — *n.* a great benefit or blessing; favor

   The new tax break has been a *boon* for small business, creating a *boom* in profits since the bill's passage.

4. choose — *v.* to pick out; to select; to make a choice
   chose — *v.* past tense of *choose*; to have selected

   Choose a color, and I'll tell you if it agrees with the color I *chose*.

5. immoral — *adj.* wicked; unchaste
   immortal — *adj.* living forever; everlasting; *n.* an immortal being

   "Remember to save your *immortal* soul in this *immoral* world," Reverend Dansey proclaimed.

6. interpret — *v.* to explain the meaning of; to understand in a particular way
   interrupt — *v.* to break in upon; to hinder

   Sorry to *interrupt*, but can you *interpret* your handwriting for me?

7. lean — *v.* to bend slightly; to slope; *adj.* not fat; meager
   lien — *n.* a legal claim on another's property for payment of a debt

   Judge Foster placed a *lien* on Harry's property because Harry's illness had depleted his *lean* bank account.

8. loose — *adj.* not fastened; slack; not shut up; not strict; *v.* to set free
   lose — *v.* to not have any longer; to fail to keep, win, get, catch

   If you set your dog *loose* at night, you'll *lose* him before morning.

9. precede — *v.* to go before in order or time; to be higher in importance
   proceed — *v.* to go on after having stopped; to advance; to take place

   Ambassador Baker will *precede* Mr. Roberts; now *proceed* into the East Room to meet the president.

10. vale — *n.* a valley
   veil — *n.* a thin material worn to protect or hide the face; anything that screens or hides

   Placing the *veil* over her face to protect it from dust, she rode her filly down into the *vale*.

Activity 21   *Business-Related Terminology—Set 2*

Regardless of your profession, you will always work with finances. This set of words concentrates on those you should know relating to financial matters.

Directions: *Learn the following 15 words and their meanings; then be prepared to write and define them as directed by your instructor.*

1. **amortization**   *n.*   the gradual reduction of a debt by means of equal-period payments sufficient to meet the current interest and principal

2. **assets**   *n.*   all items of value owned by an individual or a business

3. **compensation**   *n.*   payment; something given to make up a loss

4. **credit**   *n.*   money paid on account; permission for delayed payment

5. **debit**   *n.*   a charge against the bank account of an individual or a business

6. **dividends**   *n.*   distributed profits paid to shareholders or a corporation

7. **equity**   *n.*   the amount one's property is worth beyond what is owed on it

8. **finance charge**   *n.*   an interest charged for the use of credit covering the merchant's or banker's cost of handling the credit account

9. **interest**   *n.*   the amount paid for the use of borrowed or loaned money

10. **liabilities**   *n.*   debts or other obligations of an individual or a business

11. **mortgage**   *n.*   a legal right or claim to a piece of property given as security for a loan; *v.* to give a lender a claim to a piece of property

12. **negotiable instrument**   *n.*   an instrument such as checks, drafts, etc., signed by the maker and payable on demand to the owner for a stipulated amount of money

13. **proceeds**   *n.*   the amount of money obtained from the sale of goods or services

14. **promissory note**   *n.*   a written promise to pay a stated sum of money at a certain time to a named party

15. **security**   *n.*   bond or stock certificate; something given as a pledge indicating one will fulfill a promise

Activity 22   *Computer-Related Terminology—Set 2*

Acronyms (words formed from the first letters or syllables of a name or a series of words) and initialisms (unpronounceable letters joined from the first letters of words) are very common to computer-related vocabulary.

Directions: *Learn the following 15 acronyms and initialisms and their meanings; then be prepared to write and define them as directed by your instructor.*

1. **BASIC**   (Beginners' All-Purpose Symbolic Instruction Code) an easy-to-learn computer programming language

2. **BIOS**   (Basic Input/Output System) the system within the computer that enables the software to communicate with the hardware

3. **bit**   (binary digit) the smallest unit of information consisting of a zero or a one

4. **CAD**   (Computer-Assisted Design or Computer-Aided Design) a wide range of tools that function to expedite mechanical and electronic designs

5. **CD-ROM**   (Compact Disk Read-Only Memory) information on a disk read and accessed by a laser scanner

6. **CPU**   (Central Processing Unit) the processor and main memory of the computer

7. **CRT**   (Cathode-Ray Tube) the computer screen receiving the images as words and symbols (Although most screens now use a different technology, CRT remains the common term.)

8. **DOS**   (Disk Operating System) the underlying software that requires all other software to meet its specifications before it can be run on the computer

9. **fax**   (facsimile) picture or text images transmitted by phone lines between two locations

10. **I/O**   (Input/Output) refers to data going into and out of the CPU, required by the hardware to meet specified standards

11. **LAN**   (Local Area Network) all computers in a local geographic area, such as a department, linked via cable and served by a common file server

12. **LASER**   (Light Amplification by Stimulated Emission of Radiation) *n.* a device that generates and amplifies light waves in a narrow and extremely intense beam of light of a wavelength going in one direction; *adj.* having high-quality print output

13. **PC**   (Personal Computer) a computer that is smaller than a mainframe or minicomputer and that is operated by individuals in homes and offices

14. **RAM**   (Random-Access Memory) a temporary location in memory that lasts while processing is taking place but that is erased when the computer is powered down

15. **ROM**   (Read-Only Memory) the computer storage that is wired or burned into the computer chips as permanent memory

Directions: *Edit the following essay. Write the correct spelling of all misspelled or misused words on the blank line following each paragraph.*

Altho volumes have been writen about George Washington, little insite has been given to the biografie of one of our finest first ladys, Martha Washington.

_____

Martha Washington was born on June 2, 1731, near Williamsburg, Virginia, to excedingly rich land owners. Because of her gender and the customs of the times, Martha recieved no former scholing.

_____

At the age of seventeen, she marryed Daniel Parke Custis, a wealthy Virginia planter 13 years older than she. They had four children, two of whom dyed in child birth. Continueing vieing the elements, the other two dyed before George became president.

_____

When Martha's husband dyed in 1757, the greiving widow became one of the wealthyest women in Virginia.

_____

Her actual meeting with and engagment to George is unknown; however, we know she was eight months older than he. They were marryed on January 6, 1759.

_____

During the Revolutionary War, she journied long distances, shareing his hard ships. She joined his camp at Valley Forge during the terible winter of 1777–78, and she spent the next two winters in rouf feild conditions at his Morristown, New Jersey, camp. While there, she exceded her own expectations by organizing a women's sewing circle and mending clothes for the distraut troops.

_____

As our countries first lady, Martha suceded in managing the president's home with dignity and grace. She worked with the slaves in prepareing food and acommodations for the mansion's many guests. She controled the naturally air conditioned kitchen that adjoined the house. At the same time, she was annoied at being the first ladie and often sheid from public attention. She felt she was a state prisoner. Not wanting to be a fony, she often dressed in a wierd way for a person of her dignity, causeing many people to mistake her for the maid.

_____

_____

After George dyed in 1799, she continued to live at Mount Vernon, their lovly estate. Unfortunatly, she burned all the letters George had written to her. Think how valueable thier letters would be today.

_____

Martha Washington pased away in 1802. She is buryed at Mount Vernon by her husband's side, over looking the Potomac River.

_____

Directions: *On the blank line in each sentence, write the business-related or computer-related term described by the sentence. Then edit each sentence by drawing a line through all misspelled and misused words and writing the correct spelling directly above or directly below the incorrectly spelled or used word.*

1. Money received from any ocasion, such as a renaisance fair, in which profits accede expenses is known as _____ .

2. The basic system that enables computer hardware to interrupt the software and create paralel software and hardware functions is called _____ .

3. Despite a lean on one's home, the owner's _____, which consists of the principal already paid, is intact.

4. Each computer language contains its own grammer and programed specifications. One easy-to-learn computer language is _____ .

5. A written promise to pay a stated amount of money at a certain time, such as every two years, or biannually, is called a _____ .

6. If you chose to send a message through the telephone wires, you are sending it by _____ .

7. No sherriff will harrass you if you pay the _____ on time for using the money you borrowed.

8. A real boom to engineers working with mechanical and electronic designs is a wide range of tools known as _____ .

9. Sometimes merchants vale a _____, which is interest charged on _____, by listing a lower price; such an ommission hides added cost.

10. Although it may seem immoral because it is burned into the computer and is cancelled with great difficulty, _____ doesn't necessarily last forever.

11. Hard work generally proceeds _____, payment for services rendered.

12. Thanks to the computer's _____, no dilemna occurs between what goes in and what comes out of the computer.

13. If you loose money and incur other debts, you have accumulated a number of _____ .

14. If you plan to process letters, questionaires, and computations at home, we reccommend you purchase a _____ .

WORD STUDIES

PREFIXES

Introduction to Prefixes		38
Activity 23	Prefixes *ante-* and *anti-*	39
Activity 24	Prefixes *for-* and *fore-*	40
Activity 25	Prefixes *com-, con-, co-, col-* and *cor-*	41
Activity 26	Prefixes *de-* and *dis-*	42
Activity 27	Prefixes *en-, em-, in-* and *im-*	43
Activity 28	Prefixes *inter-, intro-,* and *intra-*	44
Activity 29	Prefixes *per-, pre-,* and *pro-*	45
Activity 30	Prefixes *non-* and *un-*	46
Activity 31	Prefixes *sub-* and *super-*	47
	Prefixes: Review	48
Activity 32	**Prefixes Signifying Numbers**	49
Activity 33	**Common Prefixes—Set 1**	50
Activity 34	**Common Prefixes—Set 2**	51
Activity 35	**Common Prefixes—Set 3**	52
Activity 36	**Spelling Words Correctly—Set 3**	53
Activity 37	**Making Sense of Word Pairs—Set 3**	54
Activity 38	**Business-Related Terminology—Set 3**	55
Activity 39	**Computer-Related Terminology—Set 3**	56
	Prefixes: Review	57
	Special Word Lists: Review	58

Part

3

Introduction to Prefixes

An effective threefold method of increasing your vocabulary comprehension is to understand (1) the meaning of the root word, (2) the meaning of the prefix, and (3) the meaning of the suffix.

A **prefix** is a syllable or syllables placed at the beginning of a root word to change the word's meaning or to form a new word. For example, you know the meaning of the words *room* and *fiction*. Now notice how this principle is applied:

■ The prefix *ante*, meaning "before," is joined to *room* to form *anteroom*, meaning the "room before," or the "room you enter before you enter the desired room."

■ The prefix *non*, meaning "not," is joined to *fiction* to form *nonfiction*, meaning the writing is "not fiction," or factual.

The activities in this part introduce several sets of related prefixes followed by a review of commonly used prefixes. Although all prefixes in the English language are not reviewed in these exercises, the common prefixes and their meanings are listed on pages 133 and 134 in the References section. Turn to those pages when you have questions concerning specific prefixes.

Before moving into the activities of this part, see how well you can apply prefixes to root words by completing the following pretest.

Directions: *From the first column, select the prefix that is best joined to the root word to provide the definition given in the third column. Write the selected prefix on the blank line in the second column.*

Prefixes	Root Word	Definition
1. anti/de/in	_____crease	to make greater or more numerous
2. im/re/trans	_____port	to carry from one place to another
3. en/in/intro	_____spection	an examination of one's thoughts and feelings
4. arch/co/super	_____angel	an angel of the highest order
5. mono/poly/tri	_____chrome	having many or various colors
6. in/non/un	_____common	rare; unusual
7. in/anti/semi	_____formal	partly formal
8. col/de/di	_____lusion	a secret agreement for a wrong purpose
9. de/pro/re	_____nounce	to speak; to declare
10. ante/post/pre	_____date	to give a date later than the actual one to something

Now check your answers: (1) increase, (2) transport, (3) introspection, (4) archangel, (5) polychrome, (6) uncommon, (7) semiformal, (8) collusion, (9) pronounce, (10) postdate.

Now you are ready to review the guidelines for prefixes.

Activity 23　Prefixes ante- *and* anti-

Because of their similarity in spelling, the prefixes *ante-* and *anti-* are often confused with each other.

Ante- means "before; in front of." Common examples of this prefix include

antechamber—a small room leading into a larger room

antedate—to place a date on something after that date has passed

antebellum—before the war, specifically the Civil War

Anti- means "against; not; opposite of; rival; counteracting." Common examples of this prefix include

anti-American—to be against America

antidepressant—a drug that fights depression

antithesis—the direct opposite of something

Further learn these prefixes by completing the following exercise, which requires you to use contextual clues (clues contained within the meaning of the sentence) to select the correct prefix.

Directions: *Using contextual clues, determine the correct prefix. Then on the blank line preceding each word, write either* ante *or* anti.

1. During World War II, the Allies used _____ aircraft as a defense against enemy planes.

2. To be used correctly, a pronoun must have an _____ cedent, consisting of a previously used noun.

3. To keep your radiator from freezing during winter months, be sure you have sufficient _____ freeze.

4. This book of _____ toxins should be used in case someone accidentally ingests poison.

5. A condition existing before birth is referred to as an _____ natal condition.

6. Your position is the _____ thesis of mine; in other words, it's directly opposite.

7. The book should have ended three chapters earlier; the actual ending is an _____ climax.

8. If you have an infection, Dr. Rolfson can give you an _____ bacterial injection.

9. The _____ body Dr. Rolfson will give you weakens the bacteria and helps your body heal.

10. You're still sneezing? Have you taken an _____ histamine?

11. What an old-fashioned, antiquated, _____ diluvian idea!

12. Meet me at eleven o'clock _____ meridiem; that's before noon.

13. Come to our party; don't be so _____ social!

14. _____ septic is used in the operating room to kill germs and prevent infection.

15. Move the couch in an _____ rior direction to position it closer to the door.

Activity 24   *Prefixes* for- *and* fore-

Although similar in spelling, the prefixes *for-* and *fore-* have very different meanings.

The prefix *for-* means "away; opposite; completely," as in

forbid—not allowed

forever—completely; without coming to an end

forsake—to give up or abandon

The prefix *fore-* means "in front of; before; beforehand," as in

forerunner—one who runs before an event

forenoon—before noon

foreground—the part in front

To further understand the difference between these two prefixes, complete the following exercise.

Directions: *Using contextual clues, determine the correct prefix. Then on the blank line preceding each word, write either* for *or* fore.

"I'll never _____give you," she screamed at her _____mer boyfriend. "That's a _____gone conclusion. You've _____saken me for another woman!"

"But I can't _____get you," he pleaded. "You're _____front in all my thoughts."

"You should have had the _____thought to think of that!" she cried. "You've _____feited your right to love me. I _____told you when we began dating that if you left me a _____lorn woman, I'd _____bid you to see me again."

"But initially I couldn't be trusted. Obviously, you could _____see I might not be true. Even so, you're _____most in my heart."

"No, take your poetry with its romantic _____word and _____close the mortgage on my heart! You're history! You're _____eign to me!" she yelled as he pounded his _____head.

"But isn't _____giveness one of your _____ordained qualities? You are _____judging me before you know the facts. You must have _____known about the great _____tune I'll inherit when I'm twenty-one. Surely my great wealth will _____tify our relationship," he begged.

"If only I could have _____seen what a rat you are!" she screamed. "If I continue a relationship with you, I can _____tell my unhappiness. I _____swear you and _____warn you to get out of my sight! _____asmuch as you try to tempt me with money, I _____cast you'll always use some _____sighted _____mula to manipulate me! I _____bid you to call me again!"

And with that remark, she turned and fled _____ward into the _____tress of her dressing room.

The _____going dialogue has a moral: Money cannot change a _____mer dirty rat into a lily white mouse.

Activity 25   Prefixes com-, con-, co-, col-, and cor-

Con-, co-, col-, and *cor-* are all variations of the prefix *com-*, which means "with; together; altogether." The following guidelines indicate the use of this prefix and its variants:

- *Com-* is typically used before *b, f, m,* and *p,* as in *combination, comfortable, commotion,* and *compile.*

- *Con-* is typically used before *c, d, f, g, j, n, q, s, t,* and *v,* as in *concoction, condition, conflict, congruence, conjunction, connection, conquest, conspire, contempt,* and *convict.*

- *Co-* is often used before vowels as well as before *h* and *gn,* as in *coaxial, coed, coherence,* and *cognate.* In addition, this spelling means "with" when joined to a number of words including *coworker* and *coeducational.*

- *Col-* is used before *l,* as in *collision* and *collection.*

- *Cor-* is used before *r,* as in *correction* and *corroborative.*

Directions: *Use the guidelines as needed to determine the correct prefix. Then on the blank line preceding each word, write* com, con, co, col, *or* cor.

1. My _____ league, Professor Wrather, has _____ lected data on the _____ plex issue and has input the data into a _____ puter database.

2. Can you _____ roborate my findings _____ cerning the _____ rosive effects of rust on _____ densers?

3. Diligently try to _____ exist with your _____ tempories by _____ senting to _____ ply with our politically _____ rect regulations.

4. The church building _____ lapsed despite the _____ fident attitude of its architect; thankfully none of the _____ gregation was inside.

5. _____ fine your _____ respondence regarding our _____ pensation plan to a _____ lection of three or less pages.

6. The _____ authors prepared a _____ cise summary of their proposed book on _____ merce in Asia.

7. We can _____ miserate with you concerning your _____ fiscated property, but we cannot officially _____ ment on it.

8. You must have sufficient tangible _____ lateral before anyone can _____ sign the note because of the _____ siderable amount you are borrowing.

9. The mayor's aide was charged with both _____ ruption and _____ spiracy to _____ mit a felony.

10. If you must _____ erce someone to do your bidding, you may be denying someone's _____ stitutional rights to _____ tentment.

Activity 26   *Prefixes de- and dis-*

Because the prefixes *de-* and *dis-* have similar meanings, they may be confused. Apply the following guidelines in using the prefixes *de-* and *dis-*, as well as the variants of *dis-*: *di-* and *dif-*.

De- has five meanings:

■ opposite of, as in *deactivate*

■ down or lower, as in *deficient*

■ away or off, as in *decrease*

■ removal of or taking away from, as in *demoralize*

■ entirely, as in *destroy*

Dis- has two meanings:

■ opposite of, lack of, or not, as in *disappear*

■ apart or away, as in *dispense*

Dif- is a variant of *dis-* and is used before *f*, as in *difficult*.

Di- is another variant of *dis-*; it is used before *b, d, l, m, n, r, s, v*, and sometimes *g* and *j*, as in *digress, directions, diminish*, and *diversion*. *Di-* should not be confused with the true prefix *di-* meaning "two or twice."

Directions: *Each of the following sentences provides a brief description or definition of a word beginning with the prefix* de- *or* dis- *or a variant of* dis-. *Read the sentence; then on the blank line preceding each word, write* de, dis, di, *or* dif.

1. A medicine that relieves congestion is a _____ congestant.

2. A person who can't be trusted is likely _____ honest.

3. One who cheats you also _____ frauds you.

4. A person whom you consider to be a little odd is _____ ferent.

5. Before store merchandise is sold, it is generally placed on _____ play.

6. To get one's attention _____ verted, you show him or her something else.

7. To tear down the reputation of a person, you _____ base his or her primary qualities.

8. I _____ fer with you when I don't agree with you.

9. To get off the subject is to _____ gress.

10. If I believe you are wrong, I likely _____ agree with your opinion.

11. If you are reduced in rank, you receive a _____ motion.

12. Another measure of length or width is another _____ mension.

13. If you don't properly brush your teeth, they will likely _____ cay.

14. If I do something that affects you negatively, I do you a _____ service.

15. After eating a big meal, you hope your _____ gestive track is working well.

WORD STUDIES

Activity 27   Prefixes en-, em-, in-, *and* im-

The prefixes *en-* and *in-* and their variants *em-* and *im-* represent different meanings. Even so, they are often mistakenly interchanged.

En- and its variant *em-* mean

- "to cause to be or make," as in *endure* and *empower*

- "to put in or put on," as in *enhance* and *emphasis*.

The variant *em-* is used before *b, m,* and *p*; and *en-* is used before most other alphabetic letters.

In- and its variant *im-* mean "not; lack of; opposite of," as in *inaccurate* and *impartial*. In addition to the variant *im-*, which is used before *b, m,* and *p*, *in-* has three other variants:

- *i-*, used before *gn*, as in *ignoble*

- *il-*, used before *l*, as in *illegal*

- *ir-*, used before *r*, as in *irreverent*

Directions: *Using contextual clues, determine the correct prefix. Then on the blank line preceding each word, write* en, em, in, im, i, il, *or* ir.

If you _____ counter an _____ rational person who _____ mediately _____ braces you with seemingly _____ resistible ideas, don't get too _____ grossed with _____ conclusive ideas until you _____ sure yourself that your thinking is _____ peccable.

Too many _____ effective ideas are _____ dorsed in an _____ stant that may lead to an _____ barrassing _____ lustration of an _____ bellished fantasy that must be _____ peached before rational thinking can occur.

Rather, _____ telligent people think through startling new ideas as they are _____ countered to check for obvious _____ accuracies. The thoughts that might be _____ revocable are _____ spected thoroughly to see if they _____ ploy measures that can stand the test of time and _____ durance. Good thoughts are _____ separable from fact and will be as effective tomorrow as they are today. On the other hand, _____ lusionary concepts should be _____ gnored soon after their _____ ception because they are _____ logical and most likely _____ proper for _____ plementation.

When you are in need of a new concept, use your _____ agination to _____ part the flow of thoughts; then seriously reject those concepts that appear _____ reversible, _____ respective of any _____ itial favorable reactions.

Once you have developed forward-looking concepts that should be _____ ployed, _____ deavor to _____ itiate your _____ portant concepts _____ mediately for your _____ thusiastic success.

Activity 28   Prefixes inter-, intro-, and intra-

Although the prefixes *inter-*, *intro-*, and *intra-* do not have identical meanings, they look very much alike and are sometimes confused.

The prefix *inter-* means

- "one with the other; together," as in *interact*

- "between or among," as in *intercede*

  Inter- is used more frequently than are *intro-* and *intra-*.
  The prefix *intro-* means

- "inward; within," as in *introduction* and *introvert*. Fewer than five commonly used words and their derivatives use this prefix.

  The prefix *intra-* means

- "within; inside; on the inside," as in *intramural* and *intrastate*. Only a few common words use this prefix.

  Although *intra-* and *intro-* have similar definitions, they are not alternate forms. *Intra-* comes from the Latin *intra* meaning "inside of," and *intro-* is derived from the Latin *intro* meaning "inwardly."

Directions: *Using contextual clues, determine the correct prefix. Then on the blank line preceding each word, write* inter, intro, *or* intra.

1. _____state-15 begins at the Canadian border on the north and ends at the Mexican border on the south.

2. Since I have a sore throat, will you _____duce our keynote speaker?

3. The computer and all its boards must _____face for the computer to operate.

4. The new gasoline tax is an _____state ordinance, effective only in New Hampshire.

5. The Secretary of the _____ior is responsible for all public lands in the United States.

6. A good job offer often results from an effective _____view.

7. An _____verted person is generally shy around everyone except close friends.

8. Because of _____party fighting, the opposition swept the election.

9. Look deep into yourself through _____spection to determine your strengths and weaknesses.

10. Use the _____lude between sessions to meet our colleagues from Brown University.

Activity 29   Prefixes per-, pre-, and pro-

The prefixes *pre-* and *pro-* are often confused because of their similar meanings. In addition, the prefixes *per-* and *pre-* are often confused because they resemble each other in appearance.

The prefix *per-* means "throughout; thoroughly; very," as in *percussion* and *perceive*.

The prefix *pre-* means "before; in front of," as in *pre-Christmas* and *pre-side*. Of the three prefixes, *pre-* is the most frequently used. When *pre-* is joined to a root word beginning with an *e*, as in *pre* and *existing*, a hyphen is generally not placed between the two *e*'s (e.g., *preexisting*). The hyphen is used, however, when the root word begins with a capital letter, such as *pre-Columbian*. In such words, the prefix *pre-* is not capitalized.

The prefix *pro-* means "forward; on the side of; in place of; acting as," as in *pro-American* and *prologue*. The same guidelines for hyphenation and capitalization that apply to *pre-* also apply to *pro-*.

Directions: *Study the words listed in the first column, noting the root words and the meanings of the prefixes. Then from the second column, select the correct definition for each word, and write the corresponding letter on the blank line at the left.*

1. _____ premise (a) to be thoroughly engrossed; (b) to determine beforehand; (c) a statement assumed to be true

2. _____ perspective (a) view in correct relation; (b) alongside of; (c) to form an opinion in advance

3. _____ precept (a) a guiding principle; (b) a predetermined notion; (c) to place in front of

4. _____ promulgate (a) to produce rapidly; (b) to move forward; (c) to proclaim formally

5. _____ pre-Easter (a) following Easter; (b) before Easter; (c) in favor of having Easter

6. _____ protagonist (a) one who follows; (b) a leading character; (c) likely to debate

7. _____ predecessor (a) one who dies before another; (b) one who lives at the same time; (c) one previously in office

8. _____ permeate (a) to spread throughout; (b) to burn thoroughly; (c) to go before

9. _____ predecease (a) to die before; (b) to move in front of; (c) to live a full life

10. _____ perpetuate (a) to live a long time; (b) to be thoroughly soaked; (c) to keep a memory alive

Activity 30   *Prefixes* non- *and* un-

Although they are not alternate forms, the prefixes *non-* and *un-* have similar meanings; as a result, usage is often unclear.

The prefix *non-* means "not; opposite of; lack of; failure of," as in *nonunion* and *nonprofitable*. The prefix *non-* should not be hyphenated unless the root word is capitalized as in *non-American*. *Non-* is a "living" prefix in that it may be used before any noun, adjective, or adverb; however, if the root word also has a form that uses the prefixes *un-*, *in-*, or *dis-*, the preferred spelling is the traditional spelling rather than the formation of a new word beginning with *non-*.

When used with adjectives and adverbs, the prefix *un-* means "not," as in *untimely* and *uncomfortable*. When used with nouns, *un-* means "the opposite of," as in *untruth* and *unsatisfactory*. *Un-* is frequently used with verbs to express the opposite of the action of the verb, as in *undone* and *unlearn*.

As with the prefix *non-*, *un-* is a living prefix that can be attached to any noun, verb, adjective, or adverb to show either the opposite of the root word or a situation that is not the same as the one described by the root word. When you consult your dictionary for assistance with words beginning with *non-* and *un-*, you will find many of the *non-* and *un-* words in special columns rather than in normal alphabetical order.

In addition to *non-* and *un-*, the prefixes *in-* and *a-* can also mean "not," as in *incomprehensible* and *atypical*.

Directions: *Using contextual clues, determine the correct prefix. Then on the blank line preceding each word, write either* non *or* un.

1. Don't try to clean up the spilled milk with _____ absorbent paper towels.

2. The earthquake created countless _____ sanitary conditions throughout the city.

3. This book is based on factual accounts, definitely _____ fiction.

4. The judge indicated he was _____ biased and will remain impartial to both sides.

5. My mother often said she had a _____ productive day, seeming to get little accomplished.

6. You know that _____ breakable vase on the mantel? Well, I just broke it.

7. Although many jobs are available, few are for _____ skilled laborers.

8. The parents' group advocated more _____ violent shows on television.

9. In the fifties, the McCarthy Commission looked for people displaying _____ American behavior.

10. The Supreme Court ruled the city ordinance _____ constitutional.

WORD STUDIES

Activity 31   Prefixes *sub-* *and* super-

The prefixes *sub-* and *super-* have almost opposite meanings, yet problems occur with the prefixes that are variants of *sub-* and *super-*. The prefix *sub-* means "under; below," as in *subway* and *submarine*. It also means "further; again," as in *subdivide* and *subheading*. An additional meaning is "near; nearly," as in *subtropical* and *subarctic*. Variants of *sub-* are

■ *suc-*, used before *c*, as in *success*

■ *suf-*, used before *f*, as in *suffer*

■ *sug-*, used before *g*, as in *suggest*

■ *sup-*, used before *p*, as in *support*

■ *sus-*, used before *c*, *p*, *s*, and *t*, as in *suspense* and *susceptible*.

The prefix *super-* means "over; above," as in *superscript* and *superimpose*. It also means "besides; further; in high proportion; exceedingly," as in *supercharge* and *superhuman*. In addition, this prefix means "surpassing; more than the usual," as in *supernatural* and *superlative*. The one variant spelling of *super-* is *sur-*, which is used before several consonants, as in *surplus* and *surmount*.

Directions: *Use the guidelines as needed to determine the correct prefix. Then on the blank line preceding each word, write* sub, super, suc, suf, sug, sup, sus, *or* sur.

1. If one is to _____tain any forward motion in the sailboat, one must have favorable winds.

2. Since we will be gone for the summer, can we _____lease our apartment for three months?

3. I'll have to check with the building _____intendent to see if such an arrangement is possible.

4. The SWAT team told the armed man to _____render his hostage and come out with his hands in the air.

5. I have a _____gestion if you want input concerning your study habits.

6. _____fice it to say, I'm not willing to let you do anything you please.

7. After months of resisting, Kathy finally _____cumbed to Rob's gentle persuasion and allowed herself to date him.

8. I _____port Rosie's plan to relieve traffic congestion.

9. Come in and see my _____computer, which can do almost anything a mainframe can do.

10. Our committee is just too large to find a solution; let's form a _____committee to propose a recommendation.

Review   *Prefixes*

This exercise reviews the prefixes introduced thus far in Part 3.

Directions: *Edit the following essay. Write the correct spelling of all misspelled words on the blank line following each paragraph.*

An issue subrounding the medical perfession that has inighted much dibate and conmotion is the susject of euthanasia, or the right of medical presonnel to intracede with life and to "pull the plug" on the surport system of the terminally ill.

_____

Part of the issue revolves around the preceived duties of the physician, who has agreed to a standard of ethics that pervides the maximum health care for an enjured or ill person.

_____

Euthanasia, however, seems to undermine these ethical standards, questioning if maximum health care encludes prelonging the life of people imcapable of expressing a clear comsent to life. Some sucgest that relieving a surfering patient is playing God, thus creating a supnatural condition.

_____

Comcurrent with physicians' rights, patients' rights must also be comsidered. Some believe the rights of patients are antinatal, thus more sacred than the rights of their attendants. Opinions comcerning patients' rights are devided. Some terminally ill patients say they have lived a good life and no longer want to conexist with pain, requesting a corection to natural law in the form of an enjection interduced into their interbody bloodstream, inabling them to die with dignity.

_____

_____

Per-life advocates difagree. They assert each patient has the right to be kept alive. Perponents believe inresponsible patients should not be allowed to refuse treatment. Although a patient's right to refuse life-surtaining treatment is widely accepted, health care perfessionals should neither help nor allow terminally ill patients to hurt themselves. To do so would undermine responsible medical care, possibly creating envoluntary euthanasia to relieve financial burdens.

_____

Lawmakers are pressured to consider legislation making euthanasia legal, enpowering physicians to honor patients' requests. Until such a law subceeds, however, euthanasia remains irlegal. Even if such a law were to be passed, even one unbinding on physicians, the Supereme Court may rule it nonconstitutional.

_____

Meantime, the pre-choice and the ante-choice stands comtinue to dibate. Few people are inpartial.

_____

The forgoing decussion provides enformation rather than asks anyone to foresake closely held opinions or to colaborate on an idea that may be disferent from the mainstream.

_____

WORD STUDIES

Activity 32   Prefixes Signifying Numbers

Several prefixes and combining forms represent numbers. If you know the number represented by the prefix, you will better understand the word's meaning. The most commonly used numerical prefixes are *mono-*, *bi-*, *di-*, and *semi-*.

The prefix *mono-* means "one; single," as in *monologue* and *monotone*.

Bi- and *di-* represent the number two. *Bi-* means "twice a; two; once every two," as in *bidirectional* and *biplane*.

Di- means "twice; double; two," as in *digraph* and *dichotomous*.

The prefix *semi-* means "exactly half; partly," as in *semiannual* and *semisweet*. As with other prefixes, *semi-* is not hyphenated unless the root word is capitalized or the root word begins with *i-*, as in *semi-invalid*. Even so, the trend is moving away from using hyphens in any word starting with *semi-*.

A **combining form** is a form of a word used with words or with other combining forms to make new words, as in the combining forms in the following table that represent numbers. Try using some of these combining forms by describing a monster with different numbers of eyes, arms, etc.

Combining Form	Meaning	Combining Form	Meaning
tri	three	sept- (septem-, septi-)	seven
quadri- (quadr-)	four	octo- (oct-, octa-)	eight
tetra-	four	deca- (dec-, dek-, deka-)	ten
penta-	five	centi-	one hundred
hexa- (hex-)	six	kilo-	one thousand
hepta- (hept-)	seven	poly-	many; more than one

Directions: *Match the definition with the word by writing the letter corresponding to the correct definition from the right column on the blank line in the left column.*

1. _____	monologue	a.	conversation with oneself
2. _____	dialogue	b.	conversation between two people
3. _____	bifocals	c.	eyeglass for one eye
4. _____	monocle	d.	glasses with two lenses
5. _____	trifocals	e.	glasses with three lenses
6. _____	biannual	f.	occurring twice a year
7. _____	decade	g.	occurring every half year
8. _____	quadrennial	h.	lasting three years
9. _____	semiannual	i.	every seven years
10. _____	septennial	j.	occurring every four years
11. _____	triennial	k.	period of ten years
12. _____	bicentennial	l.	occurring every 200 years
13. _____	decagon	m.	eight angles and sides
14. _____	hexagon	n.	ten angles and sides
15. _____	octagon	o.	five angles and sides
16. _____	pentagon	p.	three or more angles
17. _____	polygon	q.	six angles and sides
18. _____	centimeter	r.	seven metrical feet
19. _____	decameter	s.	equal to ten meters
20. _____	heptameter	t.	equal to 1/100 of a meter

Activity 33   Common Prefixes—Set 1

Refer to the list of common prefixes and their meanings on pages 133 and 134 in the References section as necessary in completing this exercise.

Directions: *Using contextual clues, determine the correct prefix from the list at the left of each sentence. Then on the blank line preceding each word, write the prefix to complete the meaning of the sentence.*

anti/de/dis
1. Your car engine sounds terrible; pour a bottle of _____ knock fluid in the gas tank.

circum/contra/retro
2. The militant was charged with smuggling _____ band and with aiding the guerrillas.

epi/hyper/hypo
3. Dr. Gurr injected the _____ dermic syringe filled with penicillin to relieve the patient's sore throat.

cata/meta/semi
4. Can't you think of something more original? "She has a heart of stone" is such a common _____ phor.

circum/post/super
5. The Congressional Medal of Honor was presented to the man's family after his death, or _____ humously.

ab/ad/fore
6. The _____ breviation for doctor of medicine is M.D.

af/ef/suf
7. I received positive _____ firmation of my stand on the position paper from our company CEO.

at/de/re
8. Please _____ tach all documentation before submitting your report to the board.

de/en/re
9. _____ ception by business personnel eventually will lead to a loss of customers.

di/intro/retro
10. If you can _____ vert Mr. Arbuckle's attention, I'll have his birthday cake placed on the table.

de/ef/in
11. With the personnel rallying around her, Hudako is a very _____ fective leader.

intra/intro/retro
12. Please _____ duce me to your friends; they're people I'd like to know.

a/extra/oc
13. Flowers are appropriate for any special _____ casion.

per/pre/re
14. _____ pare yourself to receive an announcement of great significance to the firm.

abs/con/re
15. Before the president arrives each morning, you are to _____ tract major articles from the *Wall Street Journal*.

Activity 34   Common Prefixes—Set 2

Directions: *Using contextual clues, determine the correct prefix from the list at the left of each sentence. Then on the blank line preceding each word, write the prefix to complete the meaning of the sentence.*

re/retro/super

1. Suddenly, without warning, the station's logo was _____imposed over regular programming on the television screen.

intro/os/peri

2. Members of the minority group felt _____tracized when their efforts for membership were spurned.

ob/per/re

3. After you _____tain permission, please inform the group so we can enter together.

con/inter/intra

4. The referee signaled defensive pass _____ference, nullifying the _____cepted pass.

dis/extra/hyper

5. What an _____ordinary paper! You deserve more than an A grade!

em/en/im

6. Please _____boss our company name and logo on the convention folders.

di/dia/mono

7. To improve the morale of your employees, hold an effective _____logue with each one.

bi/di/pro

8. The presidents of the two nations have signed the _____lateral agreement.

ante/anti/fore

9. Place the applicants in the _____room until I'm ready for their interviews.

an/ante/en

10. Blueprints for the building's _____nex are ready for presentation.

ex/re/sub

11. We will proceed with the housing _____division as soon as the city designates curb and gutter locations.

con/per/pro

12. Professor Richardson's lecture had a _____found effect on me.

ap/com/op

13. I had just the _____posite reaction. I thought it was boring.

hyper/hypo/in

14. This new medication claims to calm _____active children.

com/ex/re

15. After several hours, security guards successfully _____pelled the rioters.

Activity 35   Common Prefixes—Set 3

Directions: *Using contextual clues, determine the correct prefix from the list at the left of each sentence. Then on the blank line preceding each word, write the prefix to complete the meaning of the sentence.*

mis/non/un   **1.** No, you definitely have a _____ conception of our organization's purpose.

dia/para/super   **2.** Because of their immediate response and effective treatment, the _____ med-ics saved my grandfather's life.

ante/circum/peri **3.** The _____ cardium is correctly defined as the membranous sac surrounding the heart.

dis/non/un   **4.** Although I didn't do well on the exam, my teacher was _____ concerned because she knew I understood the concepts.

ac/con/de   **5.** The words, "_____ cepting the award for Don Rivers is Joan Yamashita," could not be heard over the standing ovation.

al/de/mis   **6.** You can _____ lay all your preconceived fears; here comes your family now.

cata/deca/mono   **7.** Phone the _____ log department, and see if my order has been received.

col/de/inter   **8.** Suddenly the stands _____ lapsed, dropping a mass of humanity to the grass.

cor/di/per   **9.** Edit all _____ rections with a blue pencil, and return the copy as soon as possible.

for/in/re   **10.** In this gusty wind, I can't feel us making any _____ ward progress.

ir/non/un   **11.** Don't be so _____ rational; at least listen to reason.

inter/intra/pro   **12.** Our club's basketball team won our school's _____ mural league championship.

circum/intro/retro **13.** In _____ spect, I believe we should have taken a different direction.

a/non/un   **14.** That action is so _____ typical of Sonia; she's usually so composed.

arch/hyper/ultra **15.** Senator Rodriguez is labeled as the _____ conservative of the Senate, taking a conservative stand more frequently than any other senator.

WORD STUDIES

Directions: *You should know the 20 words in this exercise. Study the spelling of each word as well as its syllabication and definition. Then be prepared to write and define each word as directed by your instructor.*

1. accidentally   ac ci den tal ly   *adv.*   occurring unintentionally; not expected

2. apparel   ap par el   *n.*   clothing; dress

3. catastrophe   ca tas tro phe   *n.*   a sudden, widespread disease; misfortune

4. colleague   col league   *n.*   a fellow worker or fellow member of an organization

5. disseminate   dis sem i nate   *v.*   to scatter widely; to spread abroad

6. efficacy   ef fi ca cy   *n.*   effectiveness; the power to produce desired results

7. emphasize   em pha size   *v.*   to stress the importance of

8. exaggerate   ex ag ge rate   *v.*   to overstate; to make something greater than it actually is

9. extension   ex ten sion   *n.*   an addition; a stretching; an additional telephone

10. impeccable   im pec ca ble   *adj.*   free from fault; not capable of sin

11. inauspicious   in aus pi cious   *adj.*   unfavorable; with signs of failure

12. innuendo   in nu en do   *n.*   an indirect hint or suggestion often meant to discredit someone

13. miscellaneous   mis cel la ne ous   *adj.*   of mixed composition; dealing with various subjects

14. oblige   o blige   *v.*   to bind by a promise or duty; to compel; to force

15. permeate   per me ate   *v.*   to penetrate; to spread through the whole

16. prerogative   pre rog a tive   *n.*   a right or privilege no one else has

17. recipient   re cip i ent   *n.*   one who receives

18. subpoena   sub poe na   *n.*   an official written order commanding a person to appear as a witness in court; *v.* to summon a person to court

19. superintendent   su per in ten dent   *n.*   a person who oversees, directs, or manages

20. unanimous   u nan i mous   *adj.*   in complete accord; agreed

Activity 37   *Making Sense of Word Pairs—Set 3*

Directions: *Carefully study each pair of words. Associate the spelling with the word, the part of speech, and the definition. Note how the word is used in the illustrative sentence. Use each word as you write a sentence to be submitted to your instructor. Be prepared to write these words as directed by your instructor.*

1. access   *n.*   the right to enter; admittance
     excess   *n.*   more than enough; an action that goes beyond what is necessary
     More than 50 people have *access* to the secured area, certainly in *excess* of the number needed.

2. advice   *n.*   counsel; suggestion; recommendation
     advise   *v.*   to counsel; to recommend
     Since you asked for my *advice*, I *advise* you to choose the second offer.

3. affect   *v.*   to produce a result on; to influence or change; to stir the feelings
     effect   *v.*   to bring about; to make happen; *n.* result; influence
     The *effect* of the television commercial should *affect* increased purchasing by consumers and *effect* our overall sales.

4. collision   *n.*   a violent striking together; clash; conflict
     collusion   *n.*   a secret agreement for fraud or deceit
     The devious *collusion* of the city officials was revealed when documents were found in the jockey box after the head-on *collision*.

5. decent   *adj.*   suitable; modest; having a good reputation
     descent   *n.*   coming down from a higher place; a downward slope
     dissent   *v.*   to think differently; to disagree; to refuse to conform; *n.* a refusal to conform
     A *decent* person like you doesn't need to *descent* into mediocrity to demonstrate your *dissent* for the president's proposal.

6. emigrant   *n.*   a person who leaves his or her country of birth to settle in another
     immigrant   *n.*   a person who comes from a foreign country to live
     My neighbors were *emigrants* from Thailand; after some delay, they were allowed to become *immigrants* into the United States.

7. foreword   *n.*   a preface; an introduction
     forward   *adv.*   ahead; *adj.* near the front; advanced; ready; *v.* to help along; *n.* a basketball, hockey, or soccer player
     In the *foreword* of his novel, James Carrigan stated he wrote to *forward* the progress of minorities in the United States.

8. perform   *v.*   to do; to put into effect; to render; to act; to work
     preform   *v.*   to shape beforehand
     Because she *preformed* all intricate movements in rehearsals, Lydia *performed* the ballet with grace and beauty.

9. persecution   *n.*   a course of periodic punishment or oppression
     prosecution   *n.*   the carrying on of a lawsuit; the side starting the action in a court of law
     A witness for the *prosecution* asked the defense attorney why she was under *persecution*, being forced to answer his questions.

10. respectfully   *adv.*   in a way such as to show respect and consideration
     respectively   *adv.*   as regards to each one of several in turn or in the order mentioned
     The attorney for the defense, the attorney for the plaintiff, and the defendant, *respectively*, *respectfully* approached the judge's bench.

Activity 38   Business-Related Terminology—Set 3

Because Part 3 has concentrated on applying prefixes to root words, the business-related words in this activity use common prefixes. Use your knowledge of the root word and the prefix to aid in learning each word.

Directions: *Learn the following 15 words and their meanings; then be prepared to write and define them as directed by your instructor.*

1. **affirmative action**   *n., adj.*   a federal policy requiring employment practices that increase employment opportunities for typically disadvantaged groups

2. **coinsurance**   *n.*   a clause in a property insurance policy requiring a specified minimum amount of insurance be taken, based on the value of the property insured

3. **commensurate**   *adj.*   in the same value or extent as the original

4. **consortium**   *n.*   a partnership; an agreement among a common group for a common purpose, such as bankers coming together to help underdeveloped countries

5. **decentralization**   *n.*   the extent to which decision-making authority and responsibility are dispersed downward rather than placed at one level

6. **depreciation**   *n.*   a decrease in the value of an asset because of age, wear, obsolescence, etc.

7. **discrimination**   *n.*   giving an advantage or disadvantage to the members of one or more groups

8. **encumbrance**   *n.*   a claim against a property that makes it less than marketable or not as acceptable to a buyer

9. **exonerate**   *v.*   to declare a person innocent of any charges

10. **foreclosure**   *n.*   a legal process in which a mortgagor is deprived of interest in property because of lack of payment

11. **indictment**   *n.*   a formal written statement charging a person with an offense

12. **insolvency**   *n.*   the inability to pay one's debts as they mature

13. **misdemeanor**   *n.*   a minor violation of the law, less serious than a felony

14. **prorate**   *v.*   to proportionately distribute funds or security

15. **unsecured loan**   *n.*   a loan made on a borrower's signature, requiring no collateral

Activity 39 Computer-Related Terminology—Set 3

Many computer terms derive their specialized meanings from adding prefixes to the root words. This activity concentrates on such terms.

Directions: *Learn the following 15 words and their meanings; then be prepared to write and define them as directed by your instructor.*

1. **abort** *v.* to discontinue a program or interface activity because of computer malfunction or operator activity

2. **access** *v.* to read, write, or update information on a disk; *n.* the specific way in which the computer addresses or directs itself to data; a single reading, writing, or updating

3. **bidirectional** *adj.* referring to a printer that prints both left to right and right to left

4. **compatible** *adj.* the ability to use software on another system without a conversion program

5. **configuration** *n.* the physical setup of a computer system

6. **debugging** *v.* finding errors in a program; *adj.* referring to tools and programs used to find errors

7. **distributed processing** *n.* a system in which processing is done and saved locally rather than on a central unit

8. **emulation** *n.* a program that allows a computer system to execute programs written for another system

9. **encryption** *n.* the changing of text into a different code to prohibit its being read and understood

10. **hypermedia** *n.* a nonlinear presentation of text, graphics, and language using advanced graphical features

11. **interconnectivity** *adj.* two or more computer systems having the ability to communicate with each other

12. **nonimpact printer** *n.* laser and ink-jet printers in which the printing ball and characters do not touch the paper

13. **nonvolatile** *adj.* memory saved when the computer is turned off

14. **programming** *n.* written instructions in a computer language; *v.* to write instructions for the computer

15. **transparent** *adj.* being able to run on a computer without the user being aware of its operation

WORD STUDIES

Review   Prefixes

Since the comclusion of World War II, the United States has been envolved in nine recessions, each varying in length from 6 months to more than 20 months.

_____

Recessions are a normal part of the business cycle and often can be forcast. A typical recession is caused by an accessive buildup of business enventories, such as computer parts or retail goods. Because of this subabundance of stock, manufacturing conpanies lay off enployees until the merchandise is reduced, thus perducing few new goods.

_____

Laid-off workers are also comsumers, who in turn purchase fewer goods and services because they have superpar funds, resulting in even less spending. Thus, the cycle continues, with less buying and more nonhappy workers losing jobs. When enventories are low enough and the workforce small enough, economic activity usually picks up and business begins to espand.

_____

The recession in the early 1990s was disferent and, in a way, inlogical. When the economy should have regenerated, business perdictions did not result. Instead, many people who had temporarily lost jobs found other work, generally below their pervious skill and pay levels. Others found part-time jobs. Still others were so dicouraged, they stopped looking for work.

_____

Several reasons account for the problems of the early 1990s, some very coplex, encluding the comtinuing shift from goods-perducing to service-perducing jobs, the amount of debt at all levels, an intranational recession, and the increasing global conpetition for imdustrial dominance.

_____

To counteract this recession, the federal government interduced a number of pergrams to effect colrective action designed to foreward purchasing power and to reduce pergrams suporting comsumer antespending. One such measure envolved making enterest payments reactive to the first of the year. Once government leaders showed dicisive action and inacted legislation to stimulate the economy, the country lifted itself out of a recession.

_____

_____

Directions: *On the blank line in each sentence, write the business-related or computer-related term described by the sentence. Then edit each sentence by drawing a line through all misspelled and misused words and writing the correct spelling directly above or directly below the incorrectly spelled or used word.*

1. A partnership among nations formed to diseminate information or to pervide aid to other countries is a _____.

2. A collusion of two computer software programs results in a catstrophe, causing the program to _____.

3. A loan made solely on one's signature or the signature of a coleague with a descent reputation and made at the perrogative of the loan officer is a(n) _____.

4. An extention of ROM that is not lost when the computer is turned off is _____ memory.

5. Negative inuendos or far less than impecable treatment that unduly emphasises or impacts minority groups is called _____.

6. Some people "accidently" and inaupicisiously read other's computer data. To avoid this, _____ changes the code to make such reading impossible.

7. The persecution obtains an _____ to obblige one suspected of being guilty to be charged with a crime.

8. A _____ program will not effect a computer user's commands nor be known to the user, but it still has the ability to permate the software as needed.

9. An access of wear and tear on equipment or aparel causes faster _____ than usual.

10. Programming errors unamimously create problems for all users, exagerating user frustration. When errors occur, I advice you to obtain _____ tools that locate and eliminate the errors.

11. The emigrant into the country was served a supoena to appear in court to testify regarding his superintendant's _____, or inability to pay.

12. The physical _____ of her computer contains a floppy drive, a hard drive, and a laser printer, respectfully.

13. To foreword the progress of minority groups, _____ action programs help worthy receipents obtain employment.

14. _____ has greater eficacy than does centralized processing because all jobs, including miscelaneous ones, are completed at the local site.

SUFFIXES

Introduction to Suffixes		60
Principles of Adding Suffixes		61
Activity 40	**Suffix -able**	63
Activity 41	**Suffix -ible**	64
Activity 42	**Suffix -ant**	65
Activity 43	**Suffix -ent**	66
Activity 44	**Suffix -ance**	67
Activity 45	**Suffix -ence**	68
Activity 46	**Suffixes -ical, -cal, -cel, and -cle**	69
Activity 47	**Suffixes -ar, -er, and -or**	70
Activity 48	**Suffixes -cian and -tian**	71
Activity 49	**Suffixes -tion and -sion**	72
Activity 50	**Suffixes -ary, -ery, and -ory**	73
	Suffixes: Review	74
Activity 51	**Suffixes -ise, -ize, and -yze**	75
Activity 52	**Suffixes -ous and -eous**	76
Activity 53	**Suffixes -ious and -uous**	77
Activity 54	**Common Suffixes**	78
Activity 55	**Spelling Words Correctly—Set 4**	79
Activity 56	**Making Sense of Word Pairs—Set 4**	80
Activity 57	**Business-Related Terminology—Set 4**	81
Activity 58	**Computer-Related Terminology—Set 4**	82
	Suffixes: Review	83
	Special Word Lists: Review	84

Part

4

Introduction to Suffixes

When you added a prefix to a root word in Part 3, you formed a new word that generally possessed a meaning different from the root word. When you add a suffix to a root word, you further define or change the part of speech of the root word.

Inflectional suffixes do not change the meaning of the root word, but provide additional information, such as indicating verb tense by adding *-d* or *-ed* or changing a singular noun to a plural noun by adding *-s*. Examples of these suffixes include

require + d = required

ship + ed = shipped

state + s = states

Derivational suffixes change the part of speech as well as enhance the meaning of the root word; for example,

child + hood = childhood

rest + less = restless

soft + est = softest

Pages 61 and 62 define noun, adjective, verb, adverb, and versatile suffixes. First, however, complete the following pretest. This pretest will help you analyze your current knowledge of suffixes.

Directions: *From the first column, select the suffix that is best joined to the root word to provide the part of speech and the definition given in the third column. Write the selected suffix on the blank line in the second column.*

	Suffixes	Root Word		Definition
1.	cy/ed/ship	bankrupt_____	*n.*	the condition of being bankrupt
2.	er/ing/ish	outland_____	*adj.*	strange; ridiculous
3.	ize/ly/y	burglar_____	*v.*	to break into a building to steal
4.	ed/ing/wise	clock_____	*adv.*	in the direction of the hands of the clock
5.	ine/ite/ness	Israel_____	*n.*	a resident of Israel
6.	ly/ness/some	whole_____	*adj.*	good for health
7.	eer/er/ing	ballad_____	*n.*	one who sings ballads
8.	er/ful/yer	law_____	*n.*	one who helps others in regards to the law
9.	ity/ly/ness	illegal_____	*adv.*	not done lawfully
10.	ed/ing/ive	regress_____	*adj.*	tending to regress or decrease

Now check your answers: (1) bankruptcy, (2) outlandish, (3) burglarize, (4) clockwise, (5) Israelite, (6) wholesome, (7) balladeer, (8) lawyer, (9) illegally, (10) regressive.

Principles of Adding Suffixes

The effect of most suffixes causes root words to become nouns, adjectives, or verbs. The next two pages show the types of suffixes; pages 135 and 136 in the References section list all commonly used suffixes and their meanings.

Noun suffixes generally mean "one who; state of; act of; smaller version of; art of; form of; group of," as in the following examples:

Suffix	Example	Definition of Noun
-age	breakage	the extent of something broken
-ance	performance	the act of doing or carrying out
-cy	captaincy	the rank of a captain
-ee	employee	one who is employed
-eer	auctioneer	one who sells goods at auctions
-ence	abstinence	the giving up of certain pleasures
-ery	cookery	the art of cooking
-hood	childhood	the state of being a child
-ion	regulation	the act of controlling; a rule or law
-ism	criticism	the art of criticizing
-ist	florist	one who works with or sells flowers
-itis	appendicitis	the state of having an inflamed appendix
-ity	personality	the individual attributes of a person
-let	booklet	a small book
-ment	entertainment	that which entertains or amuses
-ness	kindness	the quality of being kind
-oid	spheroid	the form of a sphere
-ship	friendship	the state of being a friend
-ure	failure	that which is not a success

Adjective suffixes generally mean, among other things, "full of; capable of; pertaining to; tending to; having the nature of," as in the following examples:

Suffix	Example	Definition of Adjective
-able	breakable	capable of being broken
-ar	spectacular	making a great display or show
-est	warmest	most warm
-ic	artistic	having the nature of an artist
-ish	selfish	pertaining only to one's desires
-ive	regressive	tending to regress
-less	restless	tending to be unsettled
-ous	rigorous	full of rigor

Verb suffixes generally mean, among other things, "to make; to have the characteristic of," as in the following examples:

Suffix	Example	Definition of Verb
-ed	dressed	to be clothed or adorned; to be prepared
-fy	classify	to place according to a system
-ize	idolize	to make an object of worship

Adverb suffixes generally mean "manner; direction; like; most," as in the following examples:

Suffix	Example	Definition of Adverb
-ly	slowly	in a slow manner
-ward	backward	moving in an opposite direction
-wise	clockwise	in the direction of the hands of a clock

Versatile suffixes function as more than one part of speech, as in the following examples:

Suffix	Example	Definition of Example
-al	refusal	*n.* the act of refusing or denying
	fictional	*adj.* pertaining to a story of fiction
-ant	assistant	*n.* one who assists another
	arrogant	*adj.* excessively proud or haughty
-ary	notary	*n.* one who officially notarizes
	budgetary	*adj.* pertaining to financial allotments over a period of time
-ate	advocate	*n.* one who pleads the cause of another
	immediate	*adj.* of the present time; without delay
-en	sharpen	*v.* to make sharp
	woolen	*adj.* made of wool; having to do with wool
-er	abstainer	*n.* one who abstains
	softer	*adj.* pertaining to the degree of softness
-ese	Chinese	*n.* a native of China
	Chinese	*adj.* relating to China
-ful	roomful	*n.* as many as the room will hold
	eventful	*adj.* rich in events
-ing	painting	*n.* a picture done in paint
	painting	*v.* applying paint to something
-ite	Israelite	*n.* a resident of Israel
	favorite	*adj.* pertaining to the one favored
-ory	observatory	*n.* a building equipped for viewing outer space
	exploratory	*adj.* relating to the search for discoveries
-some	twosome	*n.* a group of two people
	troublesome	*adj.* tending to make trouble; annoying
-y	jealousy	*n.* the state of being jealous
	angry	*adj.* feeling or showing anger

Activity 40   *Suffix* -able

In addition to introducing a suffix, each of the next four activities will present a spelling rule that will aid you as you apply suffixes to root words.

Spelling Rule 1. When a one-syllable word ends in a consonant preceded by a vowel, double the consonant if the suffix begins with a vowel. Do *not* double the consonant if the suffix begins with a consonant.

Root Word:	m<u>ap</u>	b<u>eg</u>	sl<u>ip</u>	b<u>ad</u>
Suffix:	-<u>i</u>ng	-<u>a</u>r	-<u>e</u>ry	-ly
Derived Word:	map<u>p</u>ing	beg<u>g</u>ar	slip<u>p</u>ery	ba<u>d</u>ly

THE SUFFIX -*ABLE*

No concrete rules govern the use of -*able* and -*ible*. Of the two suffixes, -*able* is used more frequently. Both suffixes are adjectives meaning "able to; fit to be; worthy to be."

The following illustrates several common root words and their derived words with the addition of the -*able* suffix. Notice that the spelling of some root words, particularly those ending with silent *e*, is changed upon the addition of -*able*. However, some words, such as *knowledgeable*, do not drop the final *e*, as was discussed in Part 2.

accept	acceptable	compare	comparable	cure	curable
forgive	forgivable	knowledge	knowledgeable	mix	mixable
play	playable	prefer	preferable	size	sizeable

Directions: *Applying your knowledge of the root word's meaning, define each of the following words and write the definition in your own words on the blank line to the right.*

1. absorbable _____

2. advisable _____

3. charitable _____

4. detestable _____

5. employable _____

6. equitable _____

7. flammable _____

8. justifiable _____

9. marketable _____

10. operable _____

11. reliable _____

12. taxable _____

Activity 41   *Suffix* -ible

Spelling Rule 2. The final consonant is doubled when (1) the suffix begins with a vowel, (2) the word is two syllables and ends with a single consonant, and (3) the accent remains on the final syllable. The final consonant is *not* doubled if the accent shifts from the last syllable in the new word.

Root Word:	regre<u>t</u>'	confe<u>r</u>'	confe<u>r</u>'
Suffix:	-<u>a</u>ble	-<u>e</u>d	-<u>e</u>nce
Derived Word:	regre<u>tt</u>able	confe<u>rr</u>ed	confe<u>r</u>ence

THE SUFFIX *-IBLE*

Although no definitive rules exist for using *-ible*, some basic guidelines generally apply. Generally use the suffix *-ible* (1) after words or root words ending in an *s* sound, (2) after a soft *g* sound, and (3) after the letter *t*. The spelling of root words is sometimes changed, such as dropping the final, silent *e*, when *-ible* is added. Note the following examples:

S Sound:	accessible	defensible	feasible
Soft *g*:	dirigible	eligible	tangible
After *t*:	digestible	ignitible	suggestible
Root Changes:	horrible	tangible	vincible
Others:	flexible	gullible	inedible

Directions: *Using contextual clues, determine the correct suffix. Then on the blank line following each word, write either* able *or* ible.

1. "Nothing is aud_____," the elderly gentleman complained to the audiologist. "It's just not poss_____ to hear anything."

2. The prosecutor said the defendant was despic_____, elig_____ only for a jail sentence.

3. To be more access_____, Tessie posted additional office hours and made herself more amen_____ to suggestions.

4. "More avail_____ and afford_____ housing," I replied when my representative asked our needs.

5. After counseling, the husband and wife seemed more compat_____ and were more laud_____ in their remarks to each other.

6. To be employ_____, you must be cap_____, honor_____, and reli_____.

7. All perish_____ and nondur_____ goods in the sack must be refrigerated or put in basement storage.

8. The fort proved to be invinc_____ to the attackers, who were forced to flee from their immemor_____ conquest.

9. My schedule is flex_____, so call me for help with your formid_____ assignments.

10. Please be careful; that material is flamm_____ and extremely ignit_____.

Activity 42   Suffix -ant

Spelling Rule 3. When a word ends in *e*, the *e* is retained before a suffix beginning with a consonant. The *e* is dropped before a suffix beginning with a vowel.

Root Word:	retire	pursue	televise
Suffix:	-ment	-ant	-ion
Derived Word:	retirement	pursuant	television

Many words ending in *ce* and *ge* retain the *e* before all suffixes except those beginning with *e*, *i*, or *y*. This keeps the "soft" sound of *c* or *g*. In notice + able = noticeable, the *e* keeps the *c* sound "soft." In notice + ing = noticing, the *e* is dropped because the *i* keeps the *c* "soft."

Most words ending in *dge* drop the final *e* before a suffix: acknowledge + ment = acknowledgment.

Can you provide additional examples of each of these guidelines?

THE SUFFIX *-ANT*

The suffixes *-ant* and *-ent* form adjectives and nouns. As nouns they mean "a person or thing acting as an agent." As adjectives they describe the "condition" or "act" of the verb or root word. Adjectives ending in *-ant* often have a noun form ending in *-ance*. Similarly, many adjectives ending in *-ent* have a noun form ending in *-ence*.

The following list indicates several verbs with their noun or adjective forms ending in *-ant*.

aspire	aspirant	disclaim	disclaimant	fluctuate	fluctuant
inject	injectant	irritate	irritant	lubricate	lubricant
rely	reliant	resonate	resonant	signify	significant

Directions: *Using your own words, write the definition of each of the following words on the blank line to the right. Preceding each definition, indicate if the word is a noun or an adjective.*

1. accountant _____

2. applicant _____

3. blatant _____

4. brilliant _____

5. flagrant _____

6. intolerant _____

7. malignant _____

8. occupant _____

9. pageant _____

10. radiant _____

Activity 43   Suffix -ent

Spelling Rule 4. When a word ends in y preceded by a consonant, change the y to i on the addition of all suffixes except those beginning with i. Retain the y before suffixes beginning with i. When a word ends in y preceded by a vowel, retain the y when adding a suffix.

Root Word:	beau<u>ty</u>	re<u>ly</u>	ann<u>oy</u>
Suffix:	-<u>f</u>ul	-<u>i</u>ng	-<u>a</u>nce
Derived Word:	beaut<u>if</u>ul	rel<u>yi</u>ng	anno<u>ya</u>nce

Note: Irregular verbs do not follow this rule: p<u>ay</u> = p<u>ai</u>d, s<u>ay</u> = sa<u>id</u>.

THE SUFFIX *-ENT*

The suffix *-ent* also forms nouns and adjectives, although an adjective is more common:

abhor	abhorrent	consist	consistent	correspond	correspondent
indulge	indulgent	obey	obedient	occur	occurrent

Many words ending in *-ent* do not have a separate root word. For example:

accident	decent	dissent	fluent	incident
lenient	opponent	patient	tangent	violent

Directions: *Using contextual clues, determine the correct suffix. Then on the blank line following each word, write either* ant *or* ent.

1. The adolesc_____ was charged in juvenile court for driving without a license, a flagr_____ violation.

2. People intoler_____ of others' beliefs may be accused of being arrog_____.

3. To make your writing coher_____, you must be a compet_____ writer.

4. Signific_____ findings resulted from Dr. Haslum's study of organ transpl_____ recipi_____s.

5. Hernando was hesit_____ to admit he had a pleas_____ learning experience at the page_____.

6. The vac_____ lot for sale is located next to the flouresc_____ sign near Exit 281.

7. Because of Annie's allergies, perfume is an irrit_____; it smells repugn_____ to her.

8. The nonresid _____'s int_____ is to achieve excell_____ grades and earn a scholarship to avoid out-of-state tuition.

9. Despite the eloqu_____ speech, I'm still despond_____ because of preval_____ problems at home.

10. The contest_____ appar_____ly did not understand the question and lost the grand prize.

Activity 44   Suffix -ance

Many adjectives that end in *-ant* and *-ent* also have noun forms that end in *-ance* and *-ence*. Thus, if an adjective ends in *-ant* and has a noun form, the noun will always end in *-ance*. This same principle applies to words ending in *-ent*. The noun-forming suffixes *-ance* and *-ence* mean "act of; state of." The similar endings *-ancy* and *-ency* are variant forms of *-ance* and *-ence* and have the same meaning.

The following list shows several adjectives ending in *-ant* and their noun forms ending in *-ance*:

relevant	relevance	observant	observance	tolerant	tolerance
distant	distance	hesitant	hesitance	ignorant	ignorance

The following list contains several adjectives ending in *-ant* and their noun forms ending in *-ance* and *-ancy*:

compliant	compliance	compliancy	elegant	elegance	elegancy
redundant	redundance	redundancy	reluctant	reluctance	reluctancy

Directions: *The first column contains an adjective ending in* -ant. *On the blank line to the right of each word, write (1) the noun form of the word ending in* -ance *and (2) the definition of the noun form.*

1. abundant _____

2. arrogant _____

3. compliant _____

4. extravagant _____

5. flamboyant _____

6. ignorant _____

7. irrelevant _____

8. nonchalant _____

9. resonant _____

10. vigilant _____

Activity 45   Suffix -ence

All words ending in -ence are nouns. Many of these words have adjective forms ending in -ent, although some do not. The following list contains words that do not have an -ent adjective form:

audience	cadence	conference	essence
influence	jurisprudence	occurrence	science

Many other words do possess an adjective form ending in -ent; for example,

affluent	affluence	expedient	expedience
patient	patience	violent	violence

Directions: *Using contextual clues, determine the correct suffix. Then on the blank line following each word, write either ance or ence.*

1. At your conveni_____ , please answer the correspond_____ from Mr. Gregory.

2. If you plan to be in attend_____ , use the northwest entr_____ .

3. Janette has complete confid_____ in your ability to use your influ_____ in negotiating the talks.

4. The judge granted a trial continu_____ following the courtroom disturb_____ .

5. With a lot of pati_____ and persist_____ , I finally met all requirements for my degree.

6. The ess_____ of Ms. Rosenbaum's talk is to examine the consequ_____ s of fraudul_____ before compromising your ethics.

7. Three months' sever_____ pay will be given to all employees laid off during the coming time of turbul_____ .

8. The Committee for Nonviol_____ on Television will meet at Mr. Gumby's resid_____ .

9. The defendant proclaimed his innoc_____ , claiming he had been the object of vehem_____ by his enemies.

10. The import_____ of this document cannot be enh_____ d; you must treat it with defer_____ .

11. As I entered the house, my daughter asked for her allow_____ , as if removing my coat made any differ_____ .

12. "Although you may consider it a nuis_____ , repent_____ is necessary for obedi_____ to spiritual laws," shouted the evangelist.

Activity 46 Suffixes -ical, -cal, -cel, and -cle

The word endings -ical, -cal, -cel, and -cle have similar sounds. This activity will help you differentiate the four endings.

The true suffix is -ical. The word endings -cal, -cel, and -cle are variants of the suffix -ical. Most words ending in -cal actually end in -ical; for example,

anatomical	chemical	ethical	logical	mystical
optical	political	satirical	technical	vertical

A number of other words end in -cal:

equivocal	fiscal	focal	local	vocal

The -cel ending is pronounced [səl] or [sel], which is slightly different from -ical and -cal, which are pronounced [əkəl] and [kəl], respectively. As a result, when the word is pronounced with an s sound rather than a k sound, the spelling is generally -cel. Relatively few common words end in -cel. Some of them are

cancel	excel	parcel	precancel

The ending -cle in some words means "little"; in others, this meaning does not apply; for example,

circle	cuticle	debacle	follicle	monocle
muscle	pinnacle	receptacle	recycle	tricycle

Directions: *Using contextual clues, determine the correct suffix. Then on the blank line following each word, write* ical, cal, cel, *or* cle.

1. The clown rode the unicy_____ in a cir_____ to the delight of the children.

2. Some people enjoy new age or rock music; however, I have crit_____ tastes and prefer class_____ music.

3. Auditions for vo_____ parts for the school mus_____ begin Thursday at 8 p.m.

4. Unless you pay your account to our cler_____ staff, we will can_____ your subscription.

5. The press accused the president of being polit_____ when she made the appointment prior to the end of the fis_____ year.

6. If you ex_____ at the lo_____ level, you'll likely be considered for a federal judicial appointment.

7. After his hero_____ adventures, John's recovery was considered a mira_____ by the med_____ profession.

8. Enforcing econom_____ savings and barring obsta_____s, we'll meet our budget.

9. Although the motorcy_____ spun out of control, the driver escaped with only a broken clavi_____.

10. Your vehi_____ did not pass inspection. Unless you get it repaired, we will can_____ your license.

Activity 47   *Suffixes -ar, -er, and -or*

The word endings *-ar*, *-er*, and *-or* have identical sounds. The following guide-lines will help you distinguish among these suffixes.

The suffix *-ar* often forms adjectives from nouns, although some nouns and verbs also use this ending. As an adjective, *-ar* means "of the nature of; of; belonging to."

| beggar (*n.*) | cellular (*adj.*) | molar (*n.*) | secular (*adj.*) |

The suffix *-er* often forms nouns from other nouns; it also shows the comparative degree (*warm, warmer*) of adjectives and it is used in some verbs. This ending typically means "a person or thing that; one living in; one who makes or works with; a person or thing that has; a person or thing connected with; more than."

| advertiser | broader | commuter | computer | manager |
| ouster | safer | skyscraper | warmer | youngster |

The suffix *-or* often forms nouns from verbs, although it is also used with other parts of speech. This suffix designates an agent (person, thing, or quality). It may also indicate a condition or an activity. When the final syllable of the root word is *-ate* or when the root word ends in *-ct* or *-ss*, the suffix is typically *-or*.

| advisor | ancestor | counselor | denominator | endeavor |
| operator | possessor | sponsor | traitor | visitor |

Directions: *Using contextual clues, determine the correct suffix. Then on the blank line following each word, write* ar, er, *or* or.

1. My dentist said my mol_____s, in particul_____, need extra brushing and flossing.

2. To stimulate sales, merchants package products to appeal to the fav_____ of consum_____s.

3. Doct_____, do you think a don_____ will emerge before my condition gets any worse?

4. Govern_____ Randolph is expected to sign the educat_____'s retirement bill.

5. The school registr_____ indicated Jane as the school schol_____ of this year's graduating class.

6. Jerry Sanford has been named Entertain_____ of the Year by *Stell_____ Jocul_____*, the nation's leading hum_____ magazine.

7. Please call someone to repair the comput_____ and the duplicat_____.

8. The audit_____ called the bank examin_____ and the bank manag_____ into an emergency meeting.

9. Train your binocul_____s on the players to see the faces of the vict_____s.

10. The circul_____ in today's paper contains several spectacul_____ advertis_____ specials.

WORD STUDIES

Activity 48   Suffixes -cian and -tian

The suffix -*ion*, meaning "act of; condition of being; result of," has six alternate spellings: -*cian*, -*sian*, -*tian*, -*cion*, -*sion*, and -*tion*. The endings -*sian* and -*cion* are not reviewed in these activities. -*Sian* generally represents nationalities, as in *Asian*; and -*cion* is used in only two common words, *coercion* and *suspicion*.

This activity reviews -*cian* and -*tian*, and Activity 49 presents -*tion* and -*sion*.

The word ending -*cian* commonly indicates a person trained in a specific occupation or one who is expert in a specific area; for example,

academician   beautician   magician   pediatrician   statistician

Most words ending in -*tian* are related to residents of countries or geographical areas; for example,

Egyptian   Laotian   Martian   Venetian

Directions: *Each sentence defines a word ending in* -cian *or* -tian. *On the blank line following each word, apply the correct suffix by writing either* cian *or* tian.

1. A university professor may also be known as an academi_____.

2. One living on the islands southwest of Alaska is an Aleu_____.

3. One who attractively arranges hair is a beauti_____.

4. One who practices or teaches in a clinic is a clini_____.

5. A breed of dogs is Dalma_____.

6. A doctor who excels at making diagnoses is likely called a diagnosti_____.

7. A native of Egypt is an Egyp_____.

8. One who works with electricity is an electri_____.

9. A doctor who specializes in the diseases of older people is a geriatri_____.

10. A native of Haiti is a Hai_____.

11. An undertaker is another name for a morti_____.

12. A doctor who delivers babies is an obstetri_____.

13. A professional who can prescribe glasses is an opti_____.

14. One who runs for an elected office is a politi_____.

15. One who treats his or her neighbors shabbily is said to be un-Chris_____.

Activity 49   *Suffixes -tion and -sion*

Variations of the suffix *-ion* include *-tion* and *-sion*.

The word ending *-tion*, meaning "act or process of; condition of; result of," is typically added to verbs to form nouns. *-Tion* frequently follows the sounds of p, short i [i], hard c [k], and long a [ā], as well as other sounds; for example,

assumption	ignition	deduction	designation	completion
exemption	opposition	prediction	stipulation	suggestion

The suffix *-sion* typically follows root words ending in *-ss*, *-d*, *-de*, and *-se*, as well other letters. Often the spelling of the root word is modified when *-sion* is added.

digression	allusion	extension	immersion	admission
oppression	persuasion	reprehension	revision	incision

Directions: *In the following sentences, several root words are contained in parentheses. On the blank line following each word, complete the sentence by writing the noun form of the word in parentheses. Each word will end with either -sion or -tion.*

1. I have a (confess) _____ to make. I've been in (possess) _____ of your document for two months, waiting to write a (describe) _____ of the (televise) _____'s (amplify) _____ system. I'll make (restore) _____ for my (remiss) _____ and return it Monday.

2. I've come to the (conclude) _____ that people with a (devote) _____ for (confuse) _____ and (delude) _____ of others may also be guilty of (repress) _____ of their income tax (evade) _____.

3. The man involved in the (collide) _____ had a (concuss) _____ as well as a bone (protrude) _____, requiring his surgeon to make a careful (incise) _____ after giving him a (transfuse) _____ for the (alleviate) _____ of his symptoms.

4. The Senate has instigated (ratify) _____ of the bill allowing a (restrict) _____ on (restore) _____ for parties guilty of (transgress) _____ and (omit) _____, as opposed to those guilty of acts of (commit) _____ or (repulse) _____.

5. Ms. Alagier conducted a (discuss) _____ for (consider) _____ of the constitutional amendment (revise) _____ with the (presume) _____ of (prevent) _____ of (oppose) _____ by opponents. Such a hearing will likely avoid unnecessary (stipulate) _____ or (divide) _____ among colleagues on the Senate floor.

Activity 50   Suffixes -ary, -ery, and -ory

Although the suffixes -*ary*, -*ery*, and -*ory* have similar pronunciations and related meanings, they have distinctive word origins, meaning they all came from different words and often from different languages when they were incorporated into the English language.

The suffix -*ary*, meaning "place for; collection of; person or thing that; act of doing; having the nature of; characterized by," forms nouns and adjectives. When a root word ends in -*ar*, the ending will be -*ary*.

library   sanctuary   veterinary   extraordinary   disciplinary

The suffix -*ery*, meaning "place for; art or occupation; condition of; qualities/ actions of; group of," forms nouns. When a root word ends in -*er*, the ending will be -*ery*.

bakery   pottery   flattery   mystery   fishery   wintery

The suffix -*ory*, meaning "having to do with; characterized by; serving to; inclined to; place for," forms nouns and adjectives. When a root word ends in -*or*, the ending will be -*ory*.

advisory   sensory   victory   exploratory   factory   glory

Directions: *Using contextual clues, determine the correct suffix. Then on the blank line following each word, write* ary, ery, *or* ory.

1. The changed northern bound_____ for Wasatch Element_____ School will be announced Friday by the district secret_____.

2. Judge Reinholt had the gall_____ cleared, saying the occupants had made a mock_____ of the courtroom.

3. When you go to the groc_____ store, buy cel_____ and other low-calorie foods for diet_____ consumption.

4. The insurance actu_____ indicated one benefici_____ of the will was missing in milit_____ action, forcing a judici_____ decision.

5. The legend_____ liter_____ agent has a mast_____ with words, always avoiding defamat_____ comments.

6. The robb_____ suspect has been charged with assault and batt_____ and with forg_____, proving thiev_____ never pays.

7. The prefat_____ pages of the direct_____ will contain an executive summ_____ of the author's findings.

8. An honor_____ degree will be awarded to the pioneer who advanced neurosurg_____, certainly a laudat_____ achievement.

9. The city libr_____ contains several new additions on vocabul_____ building, hist_____, and statut_____ regulations.

10. Try to get imag_____ into your paper by using an alleg_____, but without using flow_____ adjectives and illusion_____ words unknown to the reader.

Review   *Suffixes*

This exercise reviews the suffixes introduced thus far in Part 4.

Directions: *Edit the following essay. Write the correct spelling of all misspelled words on the blank line following each paragraph.*

Effective writing is a result of excellant editing. If you enjoy writing, you likely excle as an editer. On the othor hand, if you experiance misary when you write, you likely are not in possescian of good editing skills since, in most situasions, effective writing requires good revician techniques.

_____

Relevence in writing is reduced to one compositian fact: You logiclely don't want errors in your copy. An abhorrance to anyone finding inaccuracies within our delivary or our choice of vocabulery is natural to all. In fact, we are often vocel when someone hints our writing lacks perfecsion. Bettor writing, however, is achieved through the process of prewriting, writing, and rewriting.

_____

Prewriting encompasses all events leading to writing. It includes knowing your reador, gatharing all facts for your articel, choosing your ideas, and organizing the vible and relevent documents preparatary to writing.

_____

The primery goal of the writing phase is to place your thoughts on paper. Set aside sufficiant time to write the entire papor or a major sectian at one sitting. Interrupsions disrupt the thought process. As you write, don't bothor with spelling, grammer, or word choice.

_____

After writing, let your document sit for 24 hours. Avoid the temptasion to allow others to read it. This waiting period allows your writing to become "cold" and enibles you to revise it objectively.

_____

The rewriting phase is that categary of time when the true editer and logision within you appears. Read your paper first for content. During this reading, don't concern yourself with grammer or word usage. Ask yourself: Is your content complete? Is each paragraph compatable with other paragraphs? Is your writing credable?

_____

The final reading is for copyediting and requires the dedicasion of a technition. Is each sentence grammaticlely correct? Is each word spelled correctly? Did you prefer actsion verbs? Did you use correct punctuasion?

_____

When the process of prewriting, writing, and rewriting has been mastored, you'll be the bascian of knowledge, submitting an exemplery paper that results from adequate preparatian.

_____

Activity 51 Suffixes -ise, -ize, and -yze

The primary suffix -*ize* has two variant forms, -*ise* and -*yze*, that form verbs from adjectives and nouns. This suffix generally means "make; become; engage in the use of; treat or combine with." Most common words in the English language that end with the sound [iz] use the -*ize* spelling; however, the other two spellings are also used.

Several words related to specialized fields use the -*yze* word ending. However, only two common words and their derivatives use -*yze*:

    analyze   paralyze

Over 80 common words end in -*ise*; however, they tend to fall into groups of similar words. Note how often the ending -*ise* is used in words without a separate root word; for example,

    advertise   appraise   disguise   premise   supervise

The majority of common words end in -*ize*; for example,

    authorize   civilize   maximize   stabilize   subsidize

Directions: *Using contextual clues, determine the correct suffix. Then on the blank line following each word, write* ise, ize, *or* yze.

1. After you have anal_____d the documents, please organ_____ and alphabet_____ them; then

   summar_____ them in a conc_____ manner for presentation at the conference.

2. I adv_____ you to contact someone with expert_____ to prove you didn't plagiar_____ that

   author's work. However, when you present your findings in court, exerc_____ good judgment as you

   theor_____ your speculations.

3. Don't comprom_____ your principles when you advert_____ for someone to merchand_____ your

   product. Rev_____ your ad until you fully visual_____ your reader and vocal_____ your needs.

4. When the hypnotist hypnot_____d me, I was mentally paral_____d to the point I couldn't

   recogn_____ sunr_____ from sunset. My best friend, disgu_____ d in a mask, completely

   surpr_____d me.

5. This year we'll winter_____ our home, mobil_____ our warm clothing, and head south for a

   Caribbean cru_____. After the winter months, we'll return home revital_____ d and otherw_____

   rejuvenated.

Activity 52   *Suffixes -ous and -eous*

The suffix *-ous* has two variant forms: *-ious* and *-uous*. The primary suffix will be studied in this activity, along with *-eous*, which is often confused with *-ous*. The variant forms will be studied in Activity 53.

The suffix *-ous*, meaning "full of; characterized by; having the nature of; like; practicing; inclined to," forms adjectives from nouns. This suffix comes from Old French as well as from the Latin. Adjectives ending in *-ous* are pronounced with the *us* sound directly following the preceding consonant sound, as in the following examples:

anonymous   fabulous   frivolous   nervous   numerous

The suffix *-eous*, meaning "having the nature of; like," also forms adjectives and comes from Latin roots. Adjectives ending in *-eous* are usually pronounced with a distinctive long *e* followed by the *us* sound, as in the following examples:

courteous   erroneous   hideous   spontaneous

Directions: *Using contextual clues, determine the correct suffix. Then on the blank line following each word, write* ous *or* eous.

1. James made a miracul_____ recovery after moving to this mountain_____ region. He is no longer nerv_____, and the view is gorg_____.

2. If my proposal is advantag_____, rather than outrag_____, consider giving it your gener_____ endorsement.

3. An anonym_____ donor made a fortuit_____ contribution to the Elmer R. Smeed Foundation, a marvel_____ use of funds.

4. Spontan_____ expressions of grief have been vocalized on numer_____ occasions concerning the treacher_____ and horrend_____ events in our so-called progressive community.

5. The mayor sent a humor_____, but court_____, response after my miscellan_____ comments at last Tuesday's city council meeting in which I called the mayor's actions scandal_____.

6. Another day at school, another monoton_____ lecture on a frivol_____ subject in which I have no interest. But, outwardly, I appear right_____, even though inside I feel villain_____.

7. Beware of cancer_____ foods that are danger_____ to the body. They may appear glamor_____ to the appetite of the glutton_____, but they'll do more harm than good.

Activity 53   Suffixes -ious and -uous

This activity reviews the two variant forms of the suffix *-ous*: *-ious* and *-uous*.
   Adjectives ending in *-ious* are usually pronounced with a consonant plus an *us* or a *sh* sound. The *i* is generally silent in these words. Adjectives ending in *-ious* are the most numerous of the two endings.

   ambitious   delicious   gracious   malicious   suspicious

   The *-uous* ending is usually pronounced with a *u* followed by the sound of *us* or with a *yu* followed by the sound of *us*.

   conspicuous   impetuous   presumptuous   superfluous   virtuous

Directions: *Using contextual clues, determine the correct suffix. Then on the blank line following each word, write either* ious *or* uous.

1. Jon had the dub_____ honor of being the only child with a contag_____ disease in his elementary school this winter. After a stren_____ autumn, he contracted the measles.

2. Kara has been very suspic_____ since the innoc_____ incident in which her best friend frightened her.

3. I'm cur_____ as to how you make such delic_____ brownies; they're simply luxur_____. Please give me your recipe.

4. Tyler felt very conspic_____ and somewhat anx_____ as he stood silently on the stage, the target of the audience's hilar_____ jokes.

5. Being a very gregar_____ person, Rhean makes friends easily. She is never obnox_____, yet is ingen_____ at accomplishing clever tasks for her friends. On the other hand, Sarah appears dev_____ and contempt_____, showing impet_____ haste, seemingly malic_____ in getting her wants supplied.

6. Being an ambit_____ young man, Curtis is notor_____ for being tenac_____, holding fast to his stubborn ideas, even though many are superfl_____ to the subject being discussed.

7. I'm just fur_____ with my parents. We had a glor_____ vacation; then they spoil it by returning home. To be ser_____, however, every moment of our var_____ activities was prec_____.

Activity 54   *Common Suffixes*

Refer to the list of commonly used suffixes and their meanings on pages 135 and 136 in the References section as necessary in completing this exercise.

Directions: *Using contextual clues, determine the correct suffix from the list at the left of each sentence. Then on the blank line following each word, write the suffix to complete the meaning of the sentence.*

ance/ancy/ant   1. My grandfather was diagnosed as having a malign_____ in his upper chest.

ee/er/ment   2. My niece is the mayor's appoint_____ to head the development office.

ic/ical/ine   3. Auditions for the spring mus_____ start at 9 a.m. in the Green Room of the Grand Theater.

hood/ish/en   4. Don't be so child_____; grow up and act mature!

ful/ing/less   5. If you are care_____ with my heart, I'll, in turn, care less for you.

ing/ize/ule   6. The time caps_____ was placed in the cornerstone to be opened in 100 years.

able/ing/ule   7. The baby's dispos_____ diapers are in the fourth drawer.

cy/ed/ion   8. You must pay your debts to avoid declaring bankrupt_____.

cation/fy/ty   9. Please simpli_____ your directions so readers can understand them.

ing/ion/ness   10. Get adequate breath protect_____ with Brand X gum, the TV commercial guarantees.

ee/ing/let   11. The book_____ released by the Daughters of the American Revolution discusses patriotic attitudes.

age/less/ward   12. To achieve success in school, you must gain for_____ progress and avoid reverse slides.

ian/ical/ity   13. John Jakes, a prominent American fictional histor_____, has written many novels with historical settings.

en/ing/less   14. Once you get off the beat_____ path, you'll be lost on your journey through life.

ism/ize/ous   15. To avoid critic_____ of your project, first pave the way with effective public relations.

Activity 55 Spelling Words Correctly—Set 4

Directions: *You should know the 20 words in this exercise. Study the spelling of each word as well as its syllabication and definition. Then be prepared to write and define each word as directed by your instructor.*

1.	accessible	ac ces si ble	*n.* easy to reach or enter; approachable
2.	acknowledgment	ac knowl edg ment	*n.* something given or an act done to show one has received a favor or a service
3.	advantageous	ad van ta geous	*adj.* given an advantage; beneficial
4.	bankruptcy	bank rupt cy	*n.* the state of being unable to pay one's debts
5.	beneficial	ben e fi cial	*adj.* producing good; favorable
6.	coincidence	co in ci dence	*n.* the chance occurrence of two things happening at the same time
7.	colloquial	col lo qui al	*adj.* using everyday, informal speech or writing; conversational
8.	criticize	crit i cize	*v.* to find fault with; to disapprove of
9.	economical	e co nom i cal	*adj.* avoiding waste; saving; being thrifty
10.	extemporaneous	ex tem po ra ne ous	*adj.* spoken or done without preparation
11.	familiar	fa mil iar	*adj.* well-known; common; intimate
12.	fluorescent	fluo res cent	*adj.* giving off light by exposure to certain rays
13.	guarantee	guar an tee	*n.* a promise or pledge to repair or to replace a product; *v.* to make such a promise
14.	itinerary	i tin e rar y	*n.* the route or plan of travel; a guidebook for travelers
15.	maintenance	main te nance	*n.* a being supported; the keeping of something in good repair
16.	mayonnaise	may on naise	*n.* a dressing used on salads, vegetables, etc.
17.	mnemonic	mne mon ic	*adj.* intended to aid the memory
18.	occurrence	oc cur rence	*n.* an event; a happening
19.	peculiar	pe cul iar	*adj.* unusual; out of the ordinary
20.	rendezvous	ren dez vous	*n.* an appointment by mutual agreement; *v.* to meet by agreement at a fixed place or time

Directions: *Carefully study each pair of words. Associate the spelling with the word, the part of speech, and the definition. Note how the word is used in the illustrative sentence. Use each word as you write a sentence to be submitted to your instructor. Be prepared to write these words as directed by your instructor.*

1. adherence
   adherents

   n. a holding closely to; an attachment or a loyalty
   n. faithful supporters or followers
   If you choose to be *adherents* of a religious philosophy, you must express strict *adherence* to its tenants.

2. altar
   alter

   n. a sacred table; a block of stone upon which sacrifices are offered
   v. to make different; to change the appearance of; to modify
   Hoping the hearts of the gods would *alter*, allowing rain to fall, the native sacrificed the fatted ram on the *altar*.

3. bridal
   bridle

   adj. having to do with a bride or a wedding
   n. the head part of a horse's harness; *v.* to put the headgear on a horse
   Bridle the horses and hitch them to the carriage to transport the *bridal* party to the church.

4. complement
   compliment

   n. something that completes or makes perfect; *v.* to supply what lacks
   n. something good said about another; *v.* to praise
   I *compliment* you on your ability to get your team members to *complement* each other on the basketball court.

5. confidant
   confident

   n. a person trusted with one's secrets
   adj. certain; sure of oneself
   If you're my *confidant* and I tell you my innermost thoughts, I'm *confident* you'll not reveal them.

6. eminent
   imminent

   adj. outstanding; distinguished; conspicuous
   adj. likely to happen soon; about to occur
   "An earthquake along the fault is *imminent*," proclaimed the *eminent* seismologist.

7. legislator
   legislature

   n. a lawmaker; a member of a legislative body
   n. a group of people who make the laws
   Before your *legislator* goes to the state capitol for this session of the *legislature*, express your concerns.

8. ordinance
   ordnance

   n. a rule or law; an established religious ceremony
   n. military apparatus or supplies of all kinds
   The new *ordinance* passed by the legislature concerns the *ordnance* materials supplied to the state guard.

9. precedence
   precedents

   n. the going or coming before; something of greater importance
   n. actions that serve as examples for later actions
   Federal laws take *precedence* over state laws despite the *precedents* established by the Constitution.

10. principal

    principle

    adj. most important; chief; main; *n.* the chief person; the head of a school; money on which interest is paid
    n. a primary truth; a fundamental belief
    A *principle* of our household is to pay our debts in full each month, avoiding interest on the *principal*.

Activity 57   Business-Related Terminology—Set 4

Because Part 4 has concentrated on applying suffixes to root words, the business-related words in this activity use common suffixes. Use your knowledge of the root word and the suffix to aid in learning each word.

Directions: *Learn the following 15 words and their meanings; then be prepared to write and define them as directed by your instructor.*

1. **accrual**   *n.*   money or another asset that grows in value

2. **adjuster**   *n.*   one who settles a claim between the policyholder and the insuring company

3. **appreciation**   *n.*   the amount of increase in the value of an asset over a period of time

4. **clientele**   *n.*   customers, clients, or patrons of a particular company

5. **couponing**   *n.*   the offer of a reduction in price through a coupon to persuade consumers to try a product

6. **depression**   *n.*   a period of severe reduction in business activity

7. **easement**   *n.*   the right to make limited use of real property owned by another

8. **fiscal**   *adj.*   pertaining to financial matters; related to public finance

9. **guarantee**   *n.*   the promise to repair a purchased product or to refund money paid if the product is not as represented

10. **inflation**   *n.*   a sharp overall increase in prices resulting from too great an increase in the production of paper money or bank credit

11. **liquidity**   *n.*   owning cash and/or assets easily converted into cash

12. **negotiable instrument**   *n.*   an instrument, such as checks, drafts, etc., that is signed by the maker and payable on demand to the owner for a stipulated amount of money

13. **proprietor**   *n.*   one who fully owns a business

14. **receivable**   *n.*   an asset on which payment is yet to be received

15. **variance**   *n.*   the authorization to improve or develop property in a manner not authorized by zoning ordinances

Activity 58   *Computer-Related Terminology—Set 4*

Many computer terms receive their specialized meanings when suffixes are added to the root words.

Directions: *Learn the following 15 words and their meanings; then be prepared to write and define them as directed by your instructor.*

1. **addressability**   *n., adj.*   ability of the computer to address data stored in RAM

2. **application**   *n.*   a software program used on the computer

3. **asynchronous**   *adj.*   the transmission of data one character at a time in which the intervals between characters are not equal, requiring start and stop bits between each character

4. **binary**   *adj.*   relating to a numbering system used by computers comprised of zeros and ones that indicate on and off conditions

5. **buffer**   *n.*   an area of memory reserved for the temporary storage of data

6. **centralized database**   *n.*   a database in which all files are stored on one computer and accessed from remote locations

7. **connectivity**   *n., adj.*   the ability of a computer to share data with other systems

8. **cursor**   *n.*   a small hyphenlike image on the screen that indicates the position of the next character

9. **digitizer**   *n.*   a peripheral that sends position images to the computer

10. **ergonomics**   *n.*   the study of human factors related to computing

11. **initialize**   *v.*   to make a disk or a program ready to run

12. **memory resident**   *adj.*   referring to a program that remains in memory once it is loaded and even after the computer is powered down

13. **portability**   *adj.*   capable of moving from one system to other systems

14. **sort**   *v.*   to rearrange data in ascending or descending order

15. **vendor**   *n.*   the seller or manufacturer of a software package or hardware system

Review   *Suffixes*

Directions: *Edit the following essay. Write the correct spelling of all misspelled or misused words on the blank line following each paragraph.*

In the wintor of 1945, Allied armys began the discovory of the bountous network of murdereous concentrasion camps Nazi Germany had established to paralize and eradicate Europe's Jews. Forty-eight years later, on April 22, 1993, the leadors of a dozen countrys and a crowd that included survivers and their liberaters gathered in Washington, D.C., to dedicate the United States Holocaust Memorial Museum.

_____

_____

This new museum memorialyzes the approximately 11 million victims of the Holocaust that included Jews, sexual devients, Christion religeous groups, and opponants to Hitler considered as superflious polititians. In the words of the directer, this museum is designed "to tell America and the world the factual story of this most terrable event in modern histery, and to illuminate the crucial morel lessons that it entails."

_____

_____

Visiters enter the museum into the Hall of Witness, the museum's centrle space. This hall's brick walls, exposed steel, and twisted skylight initially disoriant. Displays chronical the Holocaust, beginning with the oppresian caused by the Nazis' rise to power in Germany in 1933 and their efforts to excize undesirible populatians.

_____

Several exhibits show Jewish life before their normal life was cancled by turbulance. The three-stery Tower of Faces displays photographs of Polish Jews massacred on a single day. Names of obliterated communitys are etched on the glass wall.

_____

Other displays include shoes collected from murdered people, a purple triangle on a uniform identifying a Jehovah's Witness, and identity cards worn in the concentrasion camps. Also on display is a freight car used to transport as many as 100 people on several-day journies with little water and no food, causing many to die.

_____

The itinerery ends at the Hall of Remembrence, a quiet room designed for contemplatian. Through a skylight and narrow windows, the sun casts a soft glow on the eternal flame that burns in memery of the dead.

_____

Although difficult to comprehend, the truth is inescapible. A visit will help one appreciate the historicle trials of the past and the principals of freedom guaranteed by our Constitusion.

_____

Special Word Lists

Directions: *On the blank line in each sentence, write the business-related or computer-related term described by the sentence. Then edit each sentence by drawing a line through all misspelled and misused words and writing the correct spelling directly above or directly below the incorrectly spelled or used word.*

1. A city council often passes an ordnance that will be benificial to the city's financial, or _____, policies.

2. To avoid data being altared, start and stop bits provide acknowledgment of data in _____ transmission.

3. Legistures try to relieve a _____, a severe reduction in business activity in which many _____ (full owners of business) declare bankrupcy; however, their actions are not garanteed to work.

4. A numbering system consisting of familar ones and zeros is called a _____ system.

5. In times of economicle upswings, both principle and interest tend to increase in value. This increase is known as _____.

6. Chairs that compliment your back and feet and flurescent lights that make human working conditions more favorable—the study of which is called _____.

7. _____ are generally called the customers, patrons, or adherences of a pecular, or particular, business.

8. Programs installed in the computer (that is, _____ programs) are accessable whenever the computer is on.

9. An authorization to improve or develop property, known as a _____, may be subject to precedence, the occurrance of cases determined by previous law settlements.

10. A _____, one in which all files are stored on one computer, is advantagous to companies confidant of their data security.

11. A period of _____ is eminent when too great an increase in paper money or bank credit is available.

12. If you input an itinarary, maintainance forms, or other routine documents and your input is too rapid for the computer, excess strokes are stored in a _____, an area of temporary storage.

13. You may bridal your spending when you use reductions in price offered by product manufacturers, a practice called _____.

14. When two systems rendevous successfully, appearing to be extemporanous, the systems are said to have _____.

PLURALS AND POSSESSIVES

Introduction to Plurals and Possessives		86
Activity 59	**Plurals—Set 1**	87
Activity 60	**Plurals—Set 2**	88
Activity 61	**Plurals—Set 3**	89
Activity 62	**Plurals of Irregular and Foreign Nouns**	90
Activity 63	**Collective, Singular, and Plural Nouns**	91
Activity 64	**Possessives—Set 1**	92
Activity 65	**Possessives—Set 2**	93
	Plurals and Possessives: Review	94
Activity 66	**Spelling Words Correctly—Set 5**	95
Activity 67	**Making Sense of Word Pairs—Set 5**	96
Activity 68	**Business-Related Terminology—Set 5**	97
Activity 69	**Computer-Related Terminology—Set 5**	98
	Plurals and Possessives: Review	99
	Special Word Lists: Review	100

Part

5

Introduction to Plurals and Possessives

Good news! Adding the plural form to a singular noun and adding the possessive form to a singular or plural noun or pronoun no longer need be confusing! By following the guidelines contained in this part and by applying yourself to the accompanying exercises, you will master plurals and possessives.

The following paragraphs briefly preview the principles governing plurals and possessives. Pages 87 through 93 detail these principles as well as present additional rules for total comprehension.

PLURALS

Most common nouns form their plurals simply by adding the letter *s*. If the common noun ends in the sound of *s*, *x*, *z*, *ch*, or *sh*, the plural is formed by adding *es*.

For nouns ending in *y*: If the *y* is preceded by a consonant, change the *y* to *i* and add *es* to form the plural. If the *y* is preceded by a vowel, simply add *s* to form the plural. Proper names ending in *y* form their plurals by adding *s*, regardless of the letter preceding the final *y*.

To form the plural of a compound noun, such as *attorney at law*, add an *s* to the primary word, which is *attorney* in this case.

Foreign nouns and nouns ending with *o*, *f*, and *fe* are treated differently. Principles governing these words are detailed in the following pages.

POSSESSIVES

In working with possessives, remember one cardinal rule: In showing possession, nouns *always* add an apostrophe; pronouns *never* add an apostrophe. For example, the following pronouns are possessive: *his*, *her*, *their*, *its*. Notice *its* is the possessive form; *it's* is a contraction meaning *it is* or *it has*.

Test your knowledge of plurals and possessives by completing the following pretest.

Directions: *Column 1 contains a singular noun. On the blank lines in Columns 2, 3, and 4, write the singular possessive, plural, and plural possessive of the word in Column 1. Number 0 is provided as an example.*

Singular	Singular Possessive	Plural	Plural Possessive
0. computer	computer's	computers	computers'
1. alley			
2. boss			
3. company			
4. desk			
5. dish			
6. he or she			
7. runner-up			
8. spoonful			
9. tax			
10. waltz			

Now check your answers: (1) alley's, alleys, alleys'; (2) boss's, bosses, bosses'; (3) company's, companies, companies'; (4) desk's, desks, desks'; (5) dish's, dishes, dishes'; (6) his or her, their, theirs; (7) runner-up's, runners-up, runners-up's; (8) spoonful's, spoonfuls, spoonfuls'; (9) tax's, taxes, taxes'; (10) waltz's, waltzes, waltzes'.

WORD STUDIES

Activity 59   Plurals—Set 1

Each of the next five activities presents specialized rules related to forming plurals from singular nouns. Each activity will present two to four rules, followed by several examples that apply the specified rules. An application exercise using contextual clues will then enable you to apply your learnings in sentence constructions.

Rule 1. Most Nouns
Most nouns form their plurals by adding *s*.

application	machine	creditor	printer
applications	machines	creditors	printers

Rule 2. Nouns Ending in *s, x, z, ch, sh*, and *ss*
Nouns ending in *s, x, z, ch, sh*, and *ss* form their plurals by adding *es*.

canvas	church	prefix	brush	blitz	glass
canvases	churches	prefixes	brushes	blitzes	glasses

Rule 3. Proper Nouns
Proper nouns form their plurals in the same manner as common nouns. An *s* is added to most proper nouns; but an *es* is added to proper nouns ending in *s, x, z, ch, sh*, and *ss*.

Martha	Tex	Larry	Schultz	Williams
Marthas	Texes	Larrys	Schultzes	Williamses

Directions: *Each sentence contains at least one singular noun enclosed in parentheses and followed by a blank line. On the blank line, write the plural form of the singular noun to complete the meaning of the sentence.*

1. Most nursery (rhyme) _____ have (its) _____ share of (Jack and Jill) _____.

2. Salary (bonus) _____ are awarded at Christmastime and again at the end of all fiscal (year) _____.

3. Check both (warehouse) _____ to determine the number of (computer) _____ in stock.

4. Our two real estate (office) _____ can inform you of the (duplex) _____ available in your price range.

5. (Flight) _____ have come in all day, but the one our (grandparent) _____ are on has not yet arrived.

6. We still need (tenor) _____ and (bass) _____ in our choir.

7. In this class, we have three (Eric) _____ and two (Lucy) _____.

8. The movie *Three (Stagecoach)* _____ *from Yuma* is currently being shot in (area) _____ of southern Arizona.

9. Summer is coming; I just picked three (radish) _____ from my garden.

10. The (address) _____ of our (relative) _____ are in my blue address book.

Plurals—Set 2

This activity presents three more rules for forming plurals from singular nouns.

Rule 4. Nouns Ending in y Preceded by a Consonant
Nouns ending in *y* preceded by a consonant form their plurals by changing the *y* to *i* and adding *es*.

company	hobby	story	utility
companies	hobbies	stories	utilities

Rule 5. Nouns Ending in *y* Preceded by a Vowel
Nouns ending in *y* preceded by a vowel form their plurals by adding *s*.

alley	decoy	monkey	volley
alleys	decoys	monkeys	volleys

Rule 6. Nouns Ending in *f* and *fe*
Most nouns ending in *f* and *fe* form their plurals by adding *s*. Some nouns, however, form their plurals by changing the *f* to *v* and adding *es*.

chief	safe	knife	scarf
chiefs	safes	knives	scarves

Directions: *Each sentence contains at least one singular noun enclosed in parentheses and followed by a blank line. On the blank line, write the plural form of the singular noun to complete the meaning of the sentence.*

1. Our little town has two (cafe) _____, three (attorney) _____, but only one general store.

2. He maintains three basic (belief) _____ that govern his life and the (life) _____ of his family.

3. The (academy) _____ in the tri-cities area require all freshmen to live in (dormitory) _____.

4. She presented three (brief) _____ to the judge, hoping for one or more (victory) _____ for her (plaintiff) _____.

5. "Look, Mom, no (cavity) _____," the little boy exclaimed in the toothpaste commercial.

6. The politician garnered the majority of votes from four (county) _____ but lost the rest of the state.

7. (Toy) _____ are made for children. As a result, (manufacturer) _____ want children to put pressure on parents—both husbands and (wife) _____.

8. Your home will be secure when it guards against (thief) _____ in the night and keeps the (wolf) _____ from your property.

9. Seven (day) _____ ago our cousins entered the (valley) _____ of northern California to begin (his or her) _____ new (life) _____.

10. Before going to the dance, feed the (turkey) _____, the (donkey) _____, and the (calf) _____.

WORD STUDIES

Activity 61   Plurals—Set 3

Rule 7. Nouns Ending in *o*
The plural of nouns ending in *o* preceded by a vowel is generally formed by adding *s*. The plural of most nouns ending in *o* preceded by a consonant is often formed by adding *es*, although several words add only *s*. Nouns ending in *o* that are related to music form their plurals by adding *s*.

radio	echo	potato	piano	soprano
radios	echoes	potatoes	pianos	sopranos

Rule 8. Compound Nouns
Hyphenated compound nouns and unhyphenated compound nouns are composed of two or more words but are considered as one word. These nouns form their plurals by adding *s* to the principal word. Compound nouns written as one word usually form their plurals by adding *s* to the end. When an adverb or a preposition is hyphenated as part of a compound noun, the plural is formed by adding *s* to the noun unless the adverb or the preposition is the dominant word.

built-in	brother-in-law	notary public	housewife	spoonful
built-ins	brothers-in-law	notaries public	housewives	spoonfuls

Rule 9. Letters, Signs, and Symbols
Although style manuals differ, the plural of a lowercase letter, number, sign, or symbol is typically formed by adding an apostrophe and an *s*. Plurals of uppercase letters generally do not include an apostrophe.

B	Bs	b	b's	33	33's	$	$'s

Directions: *Each sentence contains at least one singular noun enclosed in parentheses and followed by a blank line. On the blank line, write the plural form of the singular noun to complete the meaning of the sentence.*

1. The conductor asked that several (piano) _____ (cello) _____, and (piccolo) _____ be added for the (concerto) _____.

2. Summertime means (rodeo) _____ and romantic (hero) _____ on horseback.

3. Watch your (p and q) _____ in this class or you'll receive (C and D) _____ instead of (A and B) _____.

4. The winner is awarded a gold medal; all (runner-up) _____ will receive a plaque.

5. The ranch hands have asked that (water bed) _____ be placed in the (bunkhouse) _____.

6. Turn up the (audio) _____ on your (radio) _____ and hear Mae Webb and Nelson Springer play their (banjo) _____ in a program broadcast from Warner (Studio) _____.

7. All four (ex-president) _____ signed the document next to the (x) ____ by their names.

8. Both (mother-in-law) _____ inspected our new home, checking particularly for (built-in) _____.

Activity 62　Plurals of Irregular and Foreign Nouns

Two types of nouns undergo a structural change when plurals are formed: irregular nouns and foreign nouns.

Rule 10. Irregular Nouns
Irregular nouns form their plurals through structural changes within the word. When in doubt, consult a dictionary.

child	die	foot	mouse	tooth	ox
children	dice	feet	mice	teeth	oxen

Rule 11. Foreign Nouns
Foreign nouns that do not use an English spelling form their plurals by changing the final letter or letters; for example,

a changes to *ae* (seldom used)	antenna	antennae
us changes to *i*	fungus	fungi
is changes to *es*	thesis	theses
eau changes to *eaux* (seldom used)	chateau	chateaux
um changes to *a*	datum	data
on changes to *a*	criterion	criteria
ix and *ex* change to *ces*	appendix	appendices
o changes to *i* (seldom used)	graffito	graffiti

Many frequently used foreign terms use an English spelling and form their plurals by adding *s* or *es* to the singular form.

bureau	index	formula	trousseau	crocus
bureaus	indexes	formulas	trousseaus	crocuses

Directions: *Each sentence contains at least one singular noun enclosed in parentheses and followed by a blank line. On the blank line, write the plural form of the singular noun to complete the meaning of the sentence.*

1. In his study, Dr. Goodwin developed three (hypothesis) _____ , the substance of which can be developed into at least two (thesis) _____ .

2. After you have reviewed the (datum) _____ , turn your attention to the attached (memorandum) _____ concerning the needs of the (man) _____ and (woman) _____ in the military.

3. Send the release explaining the (analysis) _____ of (nucleus) _____ studies to all broadcast and print (medium) _____ .

4. The (syllabus) _____ for courses in the humanities and English (curriculum) _____ were distributed to the committee to review the two stipulated (criterion) _____ .

5. I have (thesaurus) _____ in book and computer forms, which will help solve all our word (crisis) _____ .

6. The doctors have changed their (diagnosis) _____ to introduce possibilities of (paralysis) _____ in Victor's lower body area.

7. Since cats won't do the job, we have three (goose) _____ to control (mouse) _____ on the farm.

8. Shake the (die) _____ . The winner gets new shoes for his or her (foot) _____ .

Activity 63   Collective, Singular, and Plural Nouns

Regardless of their spelling, some nouns are always singular and others are always plural. Other nouns, including collective nouns, can be either singular or plural, depending on the context of the sentence.

Rule 12. Singular Nouns
Regardless of their spelling, some nouns arc always singular in use.

  ethics   luggage   mathematics   news   wealth

Rule 13. Plural Nouns
Regardless of their spelling, some nouns are always plural in use.

  clothes   earnings   proceeds   (the) rich   trousers

Rule 14. Same Form for Singular and Plural
Some nouns use the same spelling for both the singular and the plural forms.

  athletics deer headquarters politics sheep statistics

Rule 15. Collective Nouns
Collective nouns are singular in form but refer to a group of persons or things. When the context of the sentence indicates the group is acting as a whole, the collective noun takes a singular verb. When the context emphasizes the individual members of the group, the collective noun takes a plural verb.

  class   board   committee   jury   troop

  Because all nouns introduced in this activity are either singular or plural depending on their use in the sentence, the following exercise forces you to decide the plurality of the noun and then select the correct verb.

Directions: *In each sentence, determine if the noun requires a singular or a plural verb. Cross out the incorrect verb in the parentheses.*

1. The jury (agrees/agree) on a verdict and (is/are) ready to announce it.

2. Doing aerobics (stimulates/stimulate) a person's body and (forces/force) vitality to defeat tiredness.

3. The proceeds of the auction (reflects/reflect) the great amount of enthusiasm held for valuable junk.

4. The scissors (is/are) in the top drawer next to the refrigerator.

5. The faculty (votes/vote) on the insurance benefits in a few minutes although all (is/are) doubtful of the outcome.

6. Two pieces of my luggage (was/were) scratched by baggage handlers.

7. The news in tonight's paper (is/are) not particularly good.

8. Our earnings for this year (displays/display) a steady growth.

9. Athletics (plays/play) an important role in the lives of many alumni.

10. The crowd (was/were) dispersed quickly after the authorities arrived.

Activity 64 Possessives—Set I

Activities 64 and 65 both present three rules governing the forming of possessives to show ownership. Although some maintain inanimate objects cannot possess anything, this book illustrates possession with both animate and inanimate objects.

Rule 16. Nouns Not Ending in *s*
Nouns not ending in *s* form their possessives by adding an apostrophe and an *s*.

company	expert	Theo	transparency	umbrella
company's	expert's	Theo's	transparency's	umbrella's

Rule 17. Singular Nouns Ending in *s*
Singular nouns of one syllable ending in the sound of *s* generally form their possessives by adding an apostrophe and an *s*. Singular nouns of more than one syllable ending in the sound of *s* generally form their possessives by adding an apostrophe only.

boss	Bess	business	Congress	syllabus
boss's	Bess's	business'	Congress'	syllabus'

Rule 18. Plural Nouns Ending in *s*
Plural nouns ending in *s* form their possessives by adding an apostrophe only.

automobiles	computers	ladies	brothers	vacations
automobiles'	computers'	ladies'	brothers'	vacations'

Directions: *One or more apostrophes in each of the following sentences have been omitted. On the blank line to the right of each sentence, rewrite the word or words that show possession, placing all apostrophes correctly.*

1. The childs father could not be located when the principals office called. _____

2. That textbooks authors have submitted a proposal suggesting they write a history of ladies apparel. _____

3. All of the supervisors offices will be equipped with lounge chairs for employees comfort. _____

4. The schools vocational report found Skyview High to be in violation of the Department of Educations guidelines. _____

5. The basketball players agent has agreed to all stipulations in the new contract. _____

6. The Citizens Awareness Committee provides movie reviews for all interested parents. _____

7. Did you attend Dr. Smiths presentation last week as he discussed Mrs. Martinez impact on environmental research? _____

8. The astronomy professors secretary resigned yesterday because of a dispute with the college deans staff. _____

9. The committees meeting at the Simons home begins promptly at 7:30. _____

10. That criminal attorneys fees are in a price range similar to general practitioners fees. _____

Activity 65   Possessives—Set 2

The final three rules related to forming possessives are presented in this activity.

Rule 19. Compound Nouns
Compound nouns form their possessives by adding an apostrophe and an *s* to the final word.

| attorney at law | built-in | stockholder | notaries public |
| attorney at law's | built-in's | stockholder's | notaries public's |

Rule 20. Joint and Separate Ownership
Joint ownership is indicated by adding an apostrophe and an *s* to the last noun of the two-or-more noun combination. Separate ownership is indicated by making each noun possessive.

Joint Ownership:	Bonnie and Clyde's car (one car)
	Teresa and Ramon's house (one house)
Separate Ownership:	Romeo's and Juliet's deaths (two deaths)
	Juan's and Lucia's rooms (two rooms)

Rule 21. Pronouns
Pronouns form their possessives through irregular spelling changes. An apostrophe is never used in the possessives of pronouns.

I = mine	he = his	she = hers	it = its
we = ours	you = yours	they = theirs	who = whose
what = whose	which = whose		

Directions: *Read each sentence, noting the words in parentheses. On the blank line to the right of the sentence, rewrite the words to show possession, placing all apostrophes correctly.*

1. All the (well-wisher) cards received during your illness are in the (table) basket. _____

2. (Jessica and Bill) computer has a virus. Please send someone to repair the (computer) hard disk. _____

3. Is that (he) or (she) book that was left on the desk? _____

4. (Lewis and Clark) expedition helped open the West to future colonizers. _____

5. The (teacher) contracts are in my office ready for (they) signatures. _____

6. The (winner) reward will be a $25,000 check; the (runner-up) prize will be $10,000. _____

7. The (solicitor general) mailbox is overflowing; get someone to remove (it) contents. _____

8. Because the (credit card) interest rate is 18 percent, you'll want to pay (you) full payment each month. _____

9. The (president-elect) meeting is in the ballroom. Each person should bring (he) or (she) agenda. _____

10. (Alice Bowers and Norma Leer) law firm is located on Main Street next to the (drugstore) display. _____

Directions: *Edit the following story. Write the correct spelling of the plural or possessive form on the blank line following each paragraph.*

Our popcorn and goodys purchased, we were ready for the nights big event—the playoffes between the states top-ranked men and women basketball teams.

_____

Central City populace and the alumnus of the four schools were fired up as the teams took the floor. The crowds antics were fiercely loyal, supporting their teams.

_____

In the preliminary game, the womens teams from Starlite High and Highland High contested each other. Starlite featured the Robinsons, Jane and Tina. They playing had beaten the runner-up from Dixon High by two points. Could they beat Highland High Highlanders? Highland had the states superstar in Helen Reynolds. Reynolds points in last nights game had overcome several rallys by they opponents.

_____

Janes and Tinas parent were seated in the first row on the north side, and Helen parents were in the third row on the south side. On the floor, ten potential hero were waiting to begin.

_____

One of the official threw the ball in the air, and the game began! The players had studied their syllabus and knew the criterion for success. One team scores, then the other. Helen scores in the high 20s, and Jane and Tina play like chefes preparing a banquet. Despite great play, one team has to experience a losers defeat. Although all receive A for effort, Highland High achieves the champions victory.

_____

In the final game, the mans teams from Skyline High and Hillcrest High played to be state champion. Both teams feature a high-scoring guard, each the son of rival editor in chief of competing newspapers.

_____

This game was not for childs nor for those who avoid crisis. It resembled several circus of the stars. First one team scores; then the other matchs baskets. One pulls ahead; the other equals the score.

_____

At the end, Skyline had the higher score. But the fans themselfs poured out of the arena like sheeps, knowing everyone—men and women—had contributed. The trophys were awarded to the winners; the runner-ups received watchs. But for bragging rights, Highland and Skyline were number 1s, and Starlite and Hillcrest were 2s.

_____

Activity 66   Spelling Words Correctly—Set 5

Directions: *You should know the 20 words in this exercise. Study the spelling of each word as well as its syllabication and definition. Then be prepared to write and define each word as directed by your instructor.*

1. acknowledge	ac knowl edge	*v.*	to admit the truth of; to recognize the fact of
2. adolescent	ad o les cent	*n.*	a person from about 12 to 20 years of age
3. auxiliary	aux il iar y	*adj.*	giving help or support; *n.* a person or group giving help
4. camouflage	cam ou flage	*n.*	a disguise or false appearance to conceal; *v.* to disguise
5. chaos	cha os	*n.*	very great confusion; great disorder
6. dormitory	dor mi to ry	*n.*	a building containing many sleeping rooms
7. encyclopedia	en cy clo pe di a	*n.*	sets of books providing information on all branches of knowledge; a book fully treating a topic
8. especially	es pe cial ly	*adv.*	chiefly, more than others; particularly
9. fiasco	fi as co	*n.*	a complete or ridiculous failure; a humiliating breakdown
10. government	gov ern ment	*n.*	the rule or authority over a country, state, etc.
11. grotesque	gro tesque	*adj.*	odd or unnatural in shape, appearance, etc.
12. inoculate	in oc u late	*v.*	to inject a person with a serum designed to prevent disease
13. license	li cense	*n.*	the permission given by law to do something; *v.* to permit by law
14. limousine	lim ou sine	*n.*	a large, closed automobile in which the driver is separated from passengers
15. mathematics	math e mat ics	*n.*	the science dealing with numbers, quantitative relationships, etc.
16. naive	na ive	*adj.*	simple in nature; artless
17. pastime	pas time	*n.*	a pleasant way of spending time; an amusement; a diversion
18. phenomena	phe nom e na	*n., pl.*	facts or events that can be observed
19. reminisce	rem i nisce	*v.*	to talk or think about past experiences
20. victim	vic tim	*n.*	a person, an animal, or a thing injured, destroyed, or sacrificed

Directions: *Carefully study each pair of words. Associate the spelling with the word, the part of speech, and the definition. Note how the word is used in the illustrative sentence. Use each word as you write a sentence to be submitted to your instructor. Be prepared to write these words as directed by your instructor.*

1. access   *n.*   the right to enter; an admittance
   excess   *n.*   more than is necessary; a surplus
   An *excess* of security measures was built into the *access* system to prohibit unauthorized entry.

2. brake   *n.*   a device used to stop the motion of a vehicle; *v.* to slow or stop by using the brakes
   break   *v.*   to cause to come to pieces; to damage or destroy; *n.* a crack; a broken gap
   Slamming the *brakes*, she avoided the *break* in the road.

3. canvas   *n.*   a strong cloth with a coarse weave; an oil painting
   canvass   *v.*   to go through a district asking for votes, donations, etc.; *n.* the visiting of homes to sell something, ask for votes, etc.
   I will gladly *canvass* my street for donations since the prize is a beautiful *canvas* painting.

4. capital   *n.*   the city where government is located; a business investment; funds; *adj.* involving death
   capitol   *n.*   the building in which Congress or a state legislature meets
   The demonstration will be held on the front steps of the *capitol* in the *capital* city.

5. cite   *v.*   to quote, especially an authority; to commend publicly; to summon
   sight   *v.*   to see; to aim at; *n.* the power of seeing; something seen
   site   *n.*   a location for something; *v.* to locate; to situate
   In your release, *cite* the mayor as indicating this *site* is a beautiful *sight* to behold.

6. council   *n.*   a group of people called together to give advice or to settle questions
   counsel   *n.*   carefully considered advice; consultation; *v.* to give advice
   Members of the city *council* will *counsel* any citizen needing information about the proposed mill levy raise.

7. formally   *adv.*   in a formal manner
   formerly   *adv.*   in the past; some time ago
   Miss America, *formerly* Miss South Carolina, *formally* opened the United States' exhibit.

8. later   *adj.*   more recent; comparative of *late*; *adv.* afterward
   latter   *adj.*   the second of the two; toward the end
   Ms. O'Hara and Mr. Larson, especially the *latter* person, showed up *later* than usual.

9. role   *n.*   a part played by a person or thing
   roll   *v.*   to move by turning over and over; *n.* something rolled up; a roster
   If any of you want to audition for the *role* of the butler, please sign the *roll*.

10. who's   *pron.*   the contraction of *who is* and *who has*
    whose   *pron.*   the possessive case of *who*, *what*, or *which*
    "*Who's* going to *whose* party?" he inquired.

Activity 68   Business-Related Terminology—Set 5

This activity contains business-related words frequently heard and read; the meaning, however, may not be as common as the word.

Directions: *Learn the following 15 words and their meanings; then be prepared to write and define them as directed by your instructor.*

1. **annuity**   *n.*   a contract that provides income for a specified time

2. **attest**   *v.*   to certify; to give proof or evidence of

3. **capital investment**   *n.*   an amount invested in capital, in fixed assets, or in long-term securities not easily converted into money

4. **consumer price index**   *n.*   an index showing average prices paid for a selected number of goods and services during a given period of time

5. **debenture**   *n.*   unsecured indebtedness, usually in long-term obligations

6. **deposition**   *n.*   a written testimony sworn to be true

7. **due process**   *n.*   the whole course of legal measures that, when carried out, serve to protect people and their interests

8. **flextime**   *n.*   variations in starting and quitting times of work, assuming a set number of working hours each day

9. **inside trading**   *n.*   the trading of a company's stocks by its own directors or officers of 10 percent or more of its equity

10. **intestate**   *adj.*   dying, having left no will; *n.* a person who dies without leaving a will

11. **living trust**   *n.*   a trust made during its maker's lifetime, containing stipulations concerning the chain of succession to income in the trust

12. **prime rate**   *n.*   the lowest interest rate on business loans, available only to a bank's largest customers

13. **probate**   *n.*   the official proving of a will as genuine

14. **truth in lending**   *adj.*   requiring creditors by law to state the monthly and annual percentage rates used in computing finance charges

15. **write-off**   *n.*   a tax-deductible expense caused by an uncollected debt or a bad investment

Activity 69   *Computer-Related Terminology—Set 5*

Many computer terms have evolved from the addition of new definitions to established words.

Directions: *Learn the following 15 words and their meanings; then be prepared to write and define them as directed by your instructor.*

1. **address**   *n.*   an identifiable location in the computer's memory where data is to be stored

2. **backbone**   *n.*   the main wiring inside a building to which computer networks are attached to serve workstations

3. **boot**   *v.*   (boot up) to start up a computer system, causing the operating system to be loaded into memory

4. **environment**   *n.*   the physical setup of a computer room, such as a mainframe and peripherals

5. **execute**   *v.*   to run a program; to give a command

6. **file**   *n.*   material stored as a unit on a disk

7. **gateway**   *n.*   a processor that acts as an interface between two computer networks

8. **host**   *n.*   the main computer that stores all data accessed by computers in other locations

9. **mailbox**   *n.*   electronic storage for an individual on a network or in a bulletin board

10. **map**   *v.*   to indicate the path to a file on disk or in memory

11. **memory**   *n.*   the amount of RAM available in a computer or on a disk

12. **mouse**   *n.*   a handheld device for inputting data and commands into a computer's memory

13. **platform**   *n.*   the standard of a particular company's products

14. **refresh**   *v.*   to rewrite the screen

15. **update**   *n.*   a new release of a software package

WORD STUDIES

Review   *Plurals and Possessives*

Directions: *Edit the following essay. Write the correct spelling of all misspelled or misused words on the blank line following each paragraph.*

Each year the third Monday of January is set aside in the United States as Martin Luther Kings birthday, or Human Rights Day, to honor a man who sought to bring about social, political, and economic equality for people of all nationalitys and race's.

_____

Prior to this martyrs death on April 4, 1968, in Memphis, Tennessee, Martin Luther King became the leader of the civil rights movement. Despite he many emphasis on nonviolence, the 39-year-old King died a violent death.

_____

Born January 15, 1929, in Atlanta, Georgia, King was the son and grandson of Baptist minister. Graduating from Morehouse College, he completed advanced studys at Crozer Theological Seminary and Boston University. After his ordination as a minister in 1947, he served in several churchs. After marrying Coretta Scott in 1953, he became pastor of the Dexter Avenue Baptist Church. Martins and Corettas life were centered around multithesis of church, nation, and justice.

_____

He began his civil rights crusade in 1955, boycotting bus's in Montgomery to protest the discrimination of his race having to sit in the rear of public transportation vehicles. The boycott succeeded, convincing many that such peaceful tactic could be effective.

_____

Under Kings leadership, nonviolent resistance achieved it's greatest success. He led demonstrations in many of this countries citys. Partly as a result of his efforts, member of Congresses enacted the Civil Rights Act of 1964 and the Voting Rights Act of 1965, putting tooths into equality.

_____

King rejected the concept of separatism—equal but separate right's—and fought for integration. With the resources needed during the Vietnam War, many wanted to drop the movement like hot potatos, but King had a dream to fulfill.

_____

After his untimely death, his widow, childs, and others carried his dream to the American people. Although analysis show many minoritys—both mans and womans—are still fighting for equality, much of the success is awarded to this man with a vision. Of the many holidaies celebrated, the one honoring Martin Luther King is one of the most deserving.

_____

Review   *Special Word Lists*

Directions: *On the blank line in each sentence, write the business-related or computer-related term described by the sentence. Then edit each sentence by drawing a line through all misspelled and misused words and writing the correct spelling directly above or directly below the incorrectly spelled or used word.*

1. A term representing property, goverment securities, and other large noncash items is capitol
    _____.

2. When a program is _____ ed, the operating system is acknowleged, preventing choas or a
    fisaco as the computer is readied for use.

3. A lisensed company officer whose roll is to trade company stocks—the practice of which is illegal and
    often camoflaged—is said to be engaged in _____.

4. No victum is penalized when the enter key is depressed and a computer command is _____.

5. A _____ is a written testimony by the maker, whose fully aware of its contents.

6. An electronic _____ mathmatically provides storage for an individual with the correct excess
    passwords.

7. A _____ is made during its maker's lifetime and provides certain stipula-
    tions, such as disposal of goods, including limosine disposal for family adults and adolesents.

8. The physical setup of a computer room, including auxilliary equipment and other phonomemoa, is
    known as the _____.

9. A bank's largest customers gain a brake when they borrow because they obtain loans at the discounted
    _____.

10. The main storage unit or a centralized computer, especialy the later, that holds the data is called the
    _____.

11. An index established by a counsel of experts that shows average prices for selected goods is the
    _____.

12. An identifiable location in the computer's memory, although not actually a place (such as a dorminitory)
    or a thing that can be sighted verbally, is the _____.

13. If you die _____, you'll force your relatives to canvas your possessions since no previous stipu-
    lations were made.

14. Although a _____ was formally a grotesue rodent, it's now a handheld device for inputting data
    into the computer's memory.

                       WORD STUDIES

SYNONYMS AND ANTONYMS

Introduction to Synonyms and Antonyms   102

Activity 70   **Learning Synonyms—Set 1**   103

Activity 71   **Learning Synonyms—Set 2**   104

Activity 72   **Learning Business-Related Synonyms**   105

Activity 73   **Choosing Synonyms for Common Words**   106

Activity 74   **Learning Antonyms**   107

               Synonyms and Antonyms: Review   108

Activity 75   **Spelling Words Correctly—Set 6**   109

Activity 76   **Making Sense of Word Pairs—Set 6**   110

Activity 77   **Business-Related Terminology—Set 6**   111

Activity 78   **Computer-Related Terminology—Set 6**   112

Activity 79   **Spelling Words Correctly—Set 7**   113

Activity 80   **Making Sense of Word Pairs—Set 7**   114

               Synonyms and Antonyms: Review   115

               Special Word Lists: Review   116

Part

6

Introduction to Synonyms and Antonyms

Words are often thought of in pairs—*hot* and *cold*, *stop* and *go*, *black* and *white*. These word pairs are opposites, or **antonyms**, meaning one word in the pair means the opposite of the other word. For example, *hot* is the opposite of *cold*; thus, *hot* and *cold* are antonyms.

A word that has the same meaning as another word is called a **synonym**. Although synonyms seldom come in pairs, generally they may be substituted for each other.

Although no two words have identical meanings, such words can often be interchanged in certain contexts. Substituting allows your writing and word usage to be more lively and creative rather than dull and unimaginative.

An excellent source for learning synonyms and antonyms is your thesaurus and your dictionary. First, however, complete the following pretest using only your knowledge of words and their meanings.

Directions: *The first column contains a common word. On the blank line in the second column, write a synonym of the given word. On the blank line in the third column, write an antonym of the given word.*

Word	Synonym	Antonym
1. amuse		
2. ascend		
3. before		
4. book (*v.*)		
5. brave		
6. cautious		
7. honest		
8. lazy		
9. light		
10. operate		
11. quarrel		
12. safe		
13. tired		
14. valuable		
15. wonderful		

Because several possibilities exist for each synonym and antonym, your answers may differ from those in the following paragraph. However, possible answers include (1) amuse: entertain, bore; (2) ascend: climb, descend; (3) before: previous, subsequent; (4) book: arrange, cancel; (5) brave: gallant, cowardly; (6) cautious: alert, reckless; (7) honest: trustworthy, corrupt; (8) lazy: idle, active; (9) light: brilliant, dark; (10) operate: perform, malfunction; (11) quarrel: fight, agree; (12) safe: protected, exposed; (13) tired: weary, energetic; (14) valuable: costly, cheap; (15) wonderful: fantastic, terrible.

WORD STUDIES

Activity 70   Learning Synonyms—Set 1

Although common words are very important, using the same group of words over and over makes you appear dull. When a sentence is constructed with new words, your writing breathes new life.

Although a dictionary can be used for synonym finding, a thesaurus is more effective. Review the instructions on using the thesaurus on pages 9 and 10; then use your thesaurus as needed to complete the following exercise.

Directions: *As you read the following story, note many words are in parentheses. On the blank line following each word, substitute an appropriate synonym.*

Once upon a (time) _____ , three bears (lived) _____ in a (small) _____ (house) _____ : (Father) _____ Bear, (Mother) _____ Bear, and (little) _____ Baby Bear.

One (morning) _____ Mother Bear made oatmeal that was much too (hot) _____ . While they (waited) _____ for it to (cool) _____ , they decided to go for a (short) _____ (walk) _____ in the woods.

While they were (away) _____ , a (little) _____ (young) _____ (lady) _____ (named) _____ Goldilocks (knocked) _____ at the door. (Receiving) _____ no (answer) _____ , she (boldly) _____ (opened) _____ the (door) _____ and (walked) _____ in.

Finding the oatmeal, she (tried) _____ eating from two of the bowls before she (found) _____ one that was (edible) _____ .

Feeling (tired) _____ , she (climbed) _____ the stairs where she (found) _____ a bedroom (containing) _____ three (beds) _____ . The first bed was much too (hard) _____ . The second bed was too (soft) _____ . The third bed, (although) _____ , was just (right) _____ . So she lay down and fell fast asleep.

When the three bears (returned) _____ , they (noticed) _____ the door was (ajar) _____ . Baby Bear found his oatmeal (gone) _____ . (Running) _____ upstairs, they found one of the beds (occupied) _____ . (Suddenly) _____ Baby Bear said, "Someone has been (sleeping) _____ in my bed, and here she is!"

Within an instant, Goldilocks awoke and ran from the (house) _____ before anyone could (realize) _____ what was happening.

The (moral) _____ : Don't serve (hot) _____ oatmeal.

Activity 71   Learning Synonyms—Set 2

As you use your thesaurus for synonyms, be diligent in substituting a word with the same meaning as the original word. For example, synonyms for *little* include *petite* and *unimportant*. To pay a little girl a compliment, you could say, "She is a *petite* young lady." However, you certainly would not say, "She is an *unimportant* young lady." Even though both *petite* and *unimportant* are synonyms for *little*, they have individual meanings.

Suppose you want to impress an older man by saying he looks younger than his age. Would you say, "He is certainly a *youthful*-looking gentleman"? Or would you say, "He is certainly an *immature*-looking gentleman"? Although both words are synonyms, they do not replace each other in a sentence.

Directions: *Each sentence contains a word in parentheses. On the first blank line at the right, write a synonym that could be used in place of the word in parentheses. On the second blank line, write a synonym of the word in parentheses that could not be used as a replacement in the context of the sentence.*

1. Mrs. Adams asked her attorney for legal (advice). _____   _____

2. George McGovern was considered a (liberal) presidential candidate. _____   _____

3. What a (beautiful) baby you have! _____   _____

4. That house is too (showy) for my tastes. _____   _____

5. We both have (similar) tastes in furniture. _____   _____

6. Please don't (meddle) in my affairs. _____   _____

7. Be (quiet)! You're disturbing library patrons. _____   _____

8. What a (boring) lecture! _____   _____

9. Indeed, she is a (witty) person. _____   _____

10. We need several (good) men to complete the job on time. _____   _____

11. My parents were very (thrifty). _____   _____

12. Ralph is very (deft) at his woodworking skills. _____   _____

13. Roseanne's parents have (plenty) of money. _____   _____

14. These instructions are so (vague) I don't know what to do. _____   _____

15. Can anyone (help) me with this assignment? _____   _____

WORD STUDIES

Activity 72   Learning Business-Related Synonyms

Use your thesaurus as necessary to find synonyms for business-related words.

Directions: *Each sentence contains one or more business-related terms in parentheses. On the blank line to the right of each sentence, write a synonym for each business-related word, retaining the meaning of the sentence.*

1. A balance sheet shows an organization's (assets) and (liabilities). _____

2. A (claim) designates possession of ownership. _____

3. A good (job) move often includes additional education for (advancement). _____

4. Please send me a (bill) for services rendered. _____

5. Our loyal (customers) will receive a 10 percent (discount). _____

6. A busy (executive) often requires several (secretaries). _____
_____

7. Equal (pay) for equal work is our (company's) policy. _____

8. Last year's (recession) sharply affected our (profits). _____

9. Loyal (workers) provide great service to their (bosses). _____

10. Our company (makes) computer (parts). _____

11. Gumby's Mercantile is having a (sale) on all (goods). _____

12. My former (company) is (bankrupt). _____

13. Before writing any more (checks), (adjust) the bank statement. _____

14. The enclosed list itemizes our (spendings) during the past month. _____

15. Please read the fine print in the (contract) before signing it. _____

16. Our assistant manager will (buy) all necessary supplies. _____

17. We need someone to (negotiate) between (management) and labor. _____

18. Your (dismissal) (pay) is in the blue envelope. _____

Activity 73   *Choosing Synonyms for Common Words*

To make your writing and speaking more interesting, throw in a couple of new words. This practice will amaze those around you and, at the same time, add words to your vocabulary.

Directions: *On the blank line, write a sentence that uses a synonym of the word at the left. In the sentence, describe the word's meaning so that a person unfamiliar with your new word will understand its meaning from the context of the sentence.*

1. common _____

_____

2. aware _____

_____

3. build _____

_____

4. find _____

_____

5. happy _____

_____

6. see _____

_____

7. cheap (*adj.*) _____

_____

8. cool (*adj.*) _____

_____

9. give (*v.*) _____

_____

10. hope (*n.*) _____

_____

11. look for (*v.*) _____

_____

12. overwork (*v.*) _____

_____

13. speak (*v.*) _____

_____

14. type up (*v.*) _____

_____

15. great (*adj.*) _____

_____

WORD STUDIES

Activity 74   Learning Antonyms

An antonym is a word that means exactly the opposite of another word. You already know many antonym pairs—black and white, hot and cold, hungry and full, sleepy and wide awake. Now apply your knowledge of antonyms to the following activity, using your thesaurus if needed.

Directions: *As you read the following story, note many words are in parentheses. On the blank line following each word, substitute an appropriate antonym.*

Once upon a time, an (old) _____ lady lost her (negligent) _____ father and was (persuaded) _____ to live with her (beautiful) _____ stepmother and her two (attractive) _____ stepsisters. With the (birth) _____ of her father, Cinderella was (gradually) _____ (promoted) _____ to the lowest place in the household—that of a scullery maid.

Nothing was too good for her stepsisters, nor too (substantial) _____ for Cinderella. Her sisters received (repulsive) _____ clothes; Cinderella received rags.

One day the (miserly) _____ prince announced a kingdomwide ball with the (chance) _____ of finding a (unacceptable) _____ bride to serve as the kingdom's princess. Everyone was (indifferent) _____!

On the day of the ball, Cinderella (hindered) _____ her stepmother and stepsisters (strip) _____. But when she was finished, all she had was her (sociable) _____ corner by the fireplace where she could watch the cinders.

Suddenly a light (hid) _____, and a fairy godmother appeared to the (dry-eyed) _____ girl. Before one could say "abracadabra," Cinderella had a (buggy) _____ and four (miserly) _____ attendants and was dressed in a (plain) _____ gown. The only warning: Be home before the clock strikes (noon) _____.

At the ball, the prince was very (disgusted) _____ by Cinderella. But when the clock struck 12, away she went, (gaining) _____ a glass slipper in the process. Breathless, she (crept) _____ home.

Without (blanking) _____ it, Cinderella was the talk of the kingdom. In addition, the prince wanted to (divorce) _____ that (seasoned) _____ lady.

A (narrow) _____ search was made of the kingdom. And you (forget) _____ the rest of the story. The glass slipper fit her foot (badly) _____. Despite her (kind) _____ treatment, Cinderella treated her stepmother and stepsisters with great (disdain) _____ when she became princess of the kingdom.

The moral: If the slipper (differs) _____ , (rejuvenate) _____ it.

Review   *Synonyms and Antonyms*

Directions: *As you read the following essay, you will notice the words in parentheses are followed by a blank line. Each line is preceded by either (a) or (s). Do one of the following: (1) If the letter preceding the blank line is (s), write a synonym for the word in parentheses that fits within the context of the essay. (2) If the letter preceding the blank line is (a), write an antonym for the word in parentheses.*

Born in 1820, Florence Nightingale was the (founder) (s) _____ of the nursing (profession)
(s) _____. In addition, she was one of the (weakest) (a) _____ women to (live)
(s) _____ during England's Victorian period.

The light that Florence Nightingale (unburdened) (a) _____ has come to mean care for the
(well) (a) _____, (indifference) (a) _____ for the (ordinary) (s) _____ soldier, and
(freedom) (s) _____ for women to choose their own (work) (s) _____.

Florence Nightingale was born in Florence, Italy, the city for which she was (named) (s) _____,
to (impoverished) (a) _____ British parents living (at home) (a) _____. As a (youth)
(s) _____, she enjoyed books more than (parties) (s) _____, being (indifferent) (a)
_____ to helping others. She (visited) (s) _____ sick people on her father's (estate)
(s) _____. As she (grew) (s) _____, she took over the (management) (s) _____ of
the (tiny) (a) _____ Nightingale household.

When she was 16, she (decided) (s) _____ she wanted to spend her life helping others. She
(turned down) (s) _____ suitors, (accepted) (a) _____ (parties) (s) _____, and
(spent) (s) _____ her time learning about health and reforms for the (affluent) (a) _____ and
(suffering) (s) _____.

Her family was (advocates) (a) _____ to her life calling because at that (time) (s) _____,
nurses were known as drunken women unable to care for the sick. Florence, however, set about to (change)
(s) _____ this (image) (s) _____ .

After (relinquishing) (a) _____ her (independence) (s) _____, she studied in Paris and
served in Germany. With 38 nurses, she served during the brutal war in Crimea.

Her first (hospital) (s) _____ in Crimea consisted of old Turkish barracks, (small) (a) _____
and (spotless) (a) _____. The hospital had no (cots) (s) _____, mattresses, or bandages. She
(slowly) (a) _____ set about cleaning up the place, (using) (s) _____ the men well enough
to work as well as her nurses. Florence believed every human's life was (worthless) (a) _____.
Although Florence Nightingale had many (achievements) (s) _____ , she will always be
(forgotten) (a) _____ as the founder of modern nursing.

Activity 75   Spelling Words Correctly—Set 6

Directions: *You should know the 20 words in this exercise. Study the spelling of each word as well as its syllabication and definition. Then be prepared to write and define each word as directed by your instructor.*

1. amateur	am a teur	*n.*	one who does something for pleasure rather than money; an athlete who is not a professional
2. artificial	ar ti fi cial	*adj.*	produced by human labor; not natural; imitation of the natural
3. athletics	ath let ics	*n.*	exercises in physical strength, speed, and skill; organized active games and sports
4. banquet	ban quet	*n.*	a feast; a formal dinner; an elaborate meal
5. cemetery	cem e ter y	*n.*	a graveyard; a place where the dead are buried
6. conscientious	con sci en tious	*adj.*	being careful to do what one knows is correct
7. debris	de bris	*n.*	the remains of anything broken or destroyed; ruins
8. debut	de but	*n.*	a first public appearance
9. ecstasy	ec sta sy	*n.*	rapture; a condition of great joy
10. extinct	ex tinct	*adj.*	no longer existing; no longer active
11. inaugurate	in au gu rate	*v.*	to install in office through formal ceremonies
12. knowledge	knowl edge	*n.*	what one knows; all that is known about something
13. library	li brar y	*n.*	a collection of books, periodicals, films, tapes, etc.; a building to house such a collection
14. maneuver	ma neu ver	*v.*	to scheme; to plan carefully; *n.* a planned movement of troops, ships, etc., for tactical purposes
15. museum	mu se um	*n.*	a building or room displaying a collection of specialized objects
16. nostalgic	nos tal gic	*adj.*	feeling or showing a yearning for one's past
17. particular	par tic u lar	*adj.*	considered separately; belonging to one; different from others; hard to please
18. prestige	pres tige	*n.*	a reputation based on one's achievements, associations, etc.
19. restaurant	res tau rant	*n.*	a place to buy and eat a meal
20. separate	sep a rate	*v.*	to be between; to keep apart; to divide; to disjoin; *adj.* divided; apart from others; individual

Activity 76   Making Sense of Word Pairs—Set 6

Directions: *Carefully study each pair of words. Associate the spelling with the word, the part of speech, and the definition. Note how the word is used in the illustrative sentence. Use each word as you write a sentence to be submitted to your instructor. Be prepared to write these words as directed by your instructor.*

1. **adverse**   *adj.*   unfriendly in purpose; unfavorable; harmful
   averse   *adj.*   strong dislike; unwilling
   I'm working under *adverse* conditions; I'm very *averse* to a coworker's strong perfume.

2. **allude**   *v.*   to mention in passing; to refer to indirectly
   elude   *v.*   to avoid or escape through cleverness; to evade
   Although I *allude* to the danger of your mission, you must *elude* your enemies to be successful.

3. **continual**   *adj.*   repeated many times; recurring at regular and repeated intervals
   continuous   *adj.*   uninterrupted; connected
   Although ballet requires *continual* practice, the performance seems *continuous* to an uninterested spectator.

4. **discreet**   *adj.*   wisely cautious; showing good judgment
   discrete   *adj.*   distinct from others; discontinuous
   Please be *discreet* in working with *discrete* people who believe they're better than you.

5. **explicit**   *adj.*   clearly expressed; outspoken
   implicit   *adj.*   meant but not clearly expressed; without doubting; absolute
   The instructions given about cheating were very *explicit*, although the penalties for being caught were *implicit*, with nothing really stated.

6. **imply**   *v.*   to mean without saying so; to suggest; to signify
   infer   *v.*   to find out through reasoning; to conclude
   After checking the evidence, I can *infer* who committed the crime, although I'll need to *imply* several things to trap the guilty party.

7. **liable**   *adj.*   likely; susceptible; responsible; under obligation
   libel   *n.*   a false or damaging statement or picture; *v.* to make a damaging statement
   If your suit for *libel* is unsuccessful, you're *liable* to be a victim of a countersuit.

8. **passed**   *v.*   past tense and past participle of *pass*; to have moved beyond, handed around, or gotten through or by
   past   *adj.*   gone by; ended; *n.* the time gone by; *prep.* beyond; *adv.* beyond; by
   In the *past* when I've been *passed* by for promotion, I've only murmured a few words without doing anything.

9. **rain**   *n.*   condensed water from the sky; *v.* to fall in drops
   reign   *n.*   the period of power of a ruler; the act of ruling; *v.* to rule; to prevail
   rein   *n.*   (usually *reins*) a long, narrow strap fastened to animals to guide and control them; a means of control
   The new *reins* of command were secured in the pouring *rain*, ending a bitter *reign* of terror.

10. **waist**   *n.*   the part of the human body between the ribs and the hips; the part of a garment that covers this area
    waste   *v.*   to make poor use of; to spend uselessly; to destroy; *n.* a poor use of; *adj.* not cultivated; in ruins
    Unless I *waste* a little of this food on my plate, it will go straight to my *waist*.

WORD STUDIES

Activity 77   Business-Related Terminology—Set 6

This final set contains business-related words you should know as you prepare for your profession.

Directions: *Learn the following 15 words and their meanings; then be prepared to write and define them as directed by your instructor.*

1. **appraisal**   *n.*   an estimate of the value of a property

2. **building permit**   *n.*   an authorization by local government to build, alter, or remodel property

3. **civil rights**   *n.*   the guarantee that the rights of a citizen will be defended regardless of his or her race, color, or sex

4. **deed**   *n.*   a legal instrument that, when properly executed and delivered, transfers or conveys title of real property

5. **disclosure statement**   *n.*   a statement provided borrowers showing cash price, down payment, unpaid balance, and other charges

6. **earnest money**   *n.*   a down payment of money given as evidence of good faith to binding a contract

7. **escrow**   *n.*   the depositing of money, legal instruments, or valuables with a third party to be held until certain acts are performed or conditions met

8. **garnishment**   *n.*   the withholding of a person's pay or property by legal authority in payment of a debt

9. **joint tenancy**   *n.*   a form of concurrent ownership that includes a right of survivorship on the death of one partner

10. **mutual fund**   *n.*   an investment fund that issues or buys back shares representing partial ownership of a portfolio of actively managed securities

11. **proxy**   *n.*   a person having the authority to act for another

12. **quitclaim deed**   *n.*   a legal instrument whereby the grantor transfers rights of a property to the grantee with no statement of guarantee against claims by others

13. **reverse discrimination**   *n.*   a situation where a qualified person is denied employment because of a preference given to a protected-group individual to meet affirmative action plans

14. **underwriting**   *n.*   the process by which an insurance company determines if and on what basis it will accept an application for insurance

15. **workers' compensation**   *n.*   payment made by an employer to employees for sickness and injury— and consequent loss of income—caused by unhealthy conditions or accidents on the job

Activity 78 Computer-Related Terminology—Set 6

This final set of computer-related terminology contains commonly used computer-related words you should know to be computer literate.

Directions: *Learn the following 15 words and their meanings; then be prepared to write and define them as directed by your instructor.*

1. **artificial intelligence** *n.* the field concerned with the ways computers can simulate human intelligence

2. **baud** *n.* the speed at which information flows between devices; bits sent per second on a modem

3. **beta site** *n.* a location where a new computer hardware or software product is tested

4. **clone** *n.* a piece of equipment similar in architecture and function as another system

5. **default** *n., adj.* the automatic settings obtained upon loading a program

6. **download** *v.* to transfer files from a mainframe to a personal computer; *adj.* relating to a utility that allows text to be transferred

7. **electronic filing** *n.* the process of filing tax returns using the computer

8. **file server** *n.* a computer attached to a network that manages the programs and the workstations on the network

9. **menu-driven** *adj.* relating to a program in which users access functions through menus

10. **motherboard** *n.* the main board on the computer on which other boards are installed

11. **multitasking** *n., adj.* the concurrent execution of more than one task or program

12. **protocol** *n.* the set of rules governing computer communication

13. **RAM resident** *adj.* relating to a program that stays in memory when the computer is booted (also called Terminate and Stay Resident [TSR] program)

14. **site license** *n.* a license granting multiple copies of a program to be in use at one time in one location

15. **workstation** *n.* a user's area that contains a computer and peripherals

Spelling Words Correctly—Set 7

Directions: *You should know the 20 words in this final set of spelling words. Study the spelling of each word as well as its syllabication and definition. Then be prepared to write and define each word as directed by your instructor.*

1. antique   an tique   *n.*   something belonging to an earlier age; *adj.* out of date

2. astronaut   as tro naut   *n.*   a member of the crew of a spacecraft

3. criticism   crit i cism   *n.*   unfavorable remarks or judgments; faultfinding; a critical comment or review

4. fatigue   fa tigue   *n.*   weariness caused by hard work; *v.* to make weary or tired

5. incidentally in ci den tal ly *adv.* by the way; happening along with something of more importance

6. innovate   in no vate   *v.*   to make changes; to bring in something new

7. martyr   mar tyr   *n.*   a person who chooses to die or suffer rather than renounce faith; a person who dies or is made to suffer greatly for a cause or a principle

8. masquerade   mas que rade   *v.*   to disguise oneself; *n.* a false outward show; a party at which costumes are worn

9. mediocre   me di o cre   *adj.* ordinary; neither good nor bad

10. necessity   ne ces si ty   *n.*   an extreme need; an indispensable item

11. obscene   ob scene   *adj.* impure; offending modesty or decency

12. pavilion   pa vil ion   *n.*   a building used for shelter, entertainment, or exhibits

13. plateau   pla teau   *n.*   a plain in the mountains; a level on which something is stabilized for a period

14. pneumonia   pneu mo nia   *n.*   a lung disease accompanied by pain and fever

15. pseudonym   pseu do nym   *n.*   a fictitious name used by an author

16. sophisticate so phis ti cate *v.*   to make experienced in worldly ways

17. souvenir   sou ve nir   *n.*   a keepsake; something obtained as a remembrance

18. spaghetti   spa ghet ti   *n.*   long, slender sticks made of flour and water

19. technique   tech nique   *n.*   the method or skill of an artist, composer, poet, etc.; technical skill

20. vacuum   vac u um   *n.*   an empty space without air; a cleaning instrument; *adj.* producing an empty space; *v.* to clean with a vacuum cleaner

Activity 80   *Making Sense of Word Pairs—Set 7*

Directions: *Carefully study each set of words in this final set of word pairs. Associate the spelling with the word, the part of speech, and the definition. Note how the word is used in the illustrative sentence. Use each word as you write a sentence to be submitted to your instructor. Be prepared to write these words as directed by your instructor.*

1. adjoin   *v.*   to be next to; to be in contact with
   adjourn   *v.*   to postpone; to recess; to transfer the place of meeting
   This meeting is *adjourned* until we meet in our new building that *adjoins* the city offices.

2. disburse   *v.*   to pay out; to spend
   disperse   *v.*   to scatter; to drive in different directions
   As soon as you *disperse* the unruly mob, we'll *disburse* your payment.

3. hoard   *v.*   to save and store away for future use; *n.* that which is saved and stored
   horde   *n.*   a multitude; a great company or number; a wandering tribe
   The *horde* of squirrels gathered a *hoard* of acorns for their winter supply.

4. loose   *adj.*   not fastened; slack; not shut up; not strict; *v.* to set free
   lose   *v.*   to not have any longer; to fail to keep, win, get, or catch
   You'll *lose* your dog if you let it *loose* on these streets.

5. naval   *adj.*   relating to the navy or to warships
   navel   *n.*   the mark in the middle of the abdomen; the center
   The man who was struck in the *navel* by the bullet recently joined the *naval* command.

6. sever   *v.*   to cut apart; to break off; to divide
   severe   *adj.*   very strict; harsh; without ornament
   If you continue to be *severe* with your children, you'll *sever* your good relationship
   with them.

7. soar   *v.*   to fly at great height; to rise beyond what is common; *n.* the height reached in soaring
   sore   *adj.*   causing sharp or continued pain; distressed; angry; *n.* a painful place
   When we *soar* in the glider, I get a queasy, *sore* stomach.

8. sole   *adj.*   one and only; single; *n.* the bottom part of the foot or shoe; a fish
   soul   *n.*   the spiritual part of a person; the spirit; the essential part
   Before you can save the *souls* of the homeless, you must first put *soles* on their feet.

9. statue   *n.*   an image carved or cast in stone, wood, bronze, or clay
   stature   *n.*   height; a degree or level of physical, mental, or moral growth
   statute   *n.*   a law enacted by a legislative body
   The *statute* passed by the legislature provides funds for a *statue* of our town founder,
   a person of great *stature*.

10. vice   *n.*   an evil, immoral, or wicked habit or tendency; a flaw in one's character
    vise   *n.*   a tool for holding work, having two jaws opened and closed by a screw
    No, you can't borrow my *vise*; you have this *vice* of not returning items.

Review   Synonyms and Antonyms

Directions: *Use your thesaurus as needed in completing this exercise. The following 12 statements contain two or more underlined words. Each sentence is boring because it lacks vitality and action. On the first blank line, rewrite the sentence using synonyms for the underlined words. On the second blank line, rewrite the sentence using antonyms for the underlined words. Restructure the sentences as needed to make them more lively and creative.*

1. That <u>gadget</u> is very <u>interesting</u>.

    (syn.) _____

    (ant.) _____

2. <u>Outside</u> it's <u>sunny</u> and <u>warm</u>.

    (syn.) _____

    (ant.) _____

3. The <u>test</u> was <u>quite</u> <u>easy</u>.

    (syn.) _____

    (ant.) _____

4. I have a <u>bellyache</u>; I must have <u>overeaten</u> last night.

    (syn.) _____

    (ant.) _____

5. My next-door <u>neighbor</u> is so <u>nosy</u>.

    (syn.) _____

    (ant.) _____

6. <u>Bring</u> some <u>goodies</u> with you to the <u>party</u>.

    (syn.) _____

    (ant.) _____

7. Joe <u>said</u> he <u>needs</u> to <u>fix</u> his <u>car</u>.

    (syn.) _____

    (ant.) _____

8. Florence <u>wants</u> to go shopping at the <u>mall</u>.

    (syn.) _____

    (ant.) _____

9. If you're <u>thinking</u> what I <u>think</u> you're thinking, <u>forget</u> <u>it</u>!

    (syn.) _____

    (ant.) _____

10. I'm so <u>tired</u> of working for an <u>angry</u> <u>boss</u>.

    (syn.) _____

    (ant.) _____

11. I <u>want</u> you to be <u>happy</u> in your new <u>surroundings</u>.

    (syn.) _____

    (ant.) _____

12. All of my children are so <u>smart</u>; I can't <u>say</u> <u>enough</u> about them.

    (syn.) _____

    (ant.) _____

Directions: *On the blank line in each sentence, write the business-related or computer-related term described by the sentence. Then edit each sentence by drawing a line through all misspelled and misused words and writing the correct spelling directly above or directly below the incorrectly spelled or used word.*

1. Statues have been past deeming illegal the stating or the eluding of obseen remarks violating people's
   _____.

2. Although not served in resturants as spagetti is, these menus are involved in programs that are
   _____.

3. Time waisted because of sever injuries acquired on the job is paid through _____.

4. A place for testing new seperate programs or a librery of programs making a debue is called a
   _____.

5. _____ is a down payment promising to purchase property that you will, of
   necessety, loose if you don't fulfill your agreement.

6. A computer that runs programs meant soully for other computers may seem artifical; however, this
   second computer masqueredes as the brand-name computer and is called a _____.

7. You may be soar, but when _____ occurs, someone from a discreet
   minority group gets the job for which you're more qualified.

8. _____ is the speed at which continual data is sent through telephone lines from one computer
   to a particuler computer receiving the data.

9. Incidently, inovation and creativity in construction are not prohibited technikes if you have a
   _____ even if your new building adjourns an existing building.

10. A navel base may _____ information from the main computer in the Pentagon.

11. Funds are dispersed to a conscientous third party with presstige when funds are placed in
    _____.

12. It's not a vise and no one is libel to offer critism, but the _____ settings occur when a program
    is loaded.

13. Instructions need to be very implicit and not infer any undesired fact when a
    _____ is signed because this document transfers rights with
    no guarantee against claims.

14. Although the IRS still rains supreme, with _____ you have the knowlege
    to file your tax returns through the computer.

REVIEW EXERCISES

Posttest Review   118

Review of Part 1   119

Review of Part 2   120

Review of Part 3   121

Review of Part 4   122

Review of Part 5   123

Review of Part 6   124

Review of Spelling Words Correctly   125

Review of Making Sense of Word Pairs   126

Review of Business-Related Terminology   127

Review of Computer-Related Terminology   128

Part

7

Posttest Review

The exercises in this part provide one more opportunity to review and apply the guidelines presented in this book. Although each of the six parts is reviewed separately on the following pages, this posttest review consolidates guidelines from all six parts. Can you effectively apply the guidelines as you complete the following exercise?

   After you complete this exercise, check the answers with your instructor; then study the rules and pages in this book that review the concepts that caused you difficulty.

Directions: *On the blank line to the right of each sentence, write the correct spelling of all misspelled words.*

1. Let's procede to do the write thing at today's procedings. _____

2. Althou he died in momentary disgrace, his epitaf should reflect his many accomplishments. _____

3. Circleing the airport, the airplane began loosing fuel and made a rapid decent. _____

4. Being annoied at the slowness of action on the treatys, the foriegn diplomat requested a more efficeint system. _____

5. Being antewar, she demonstrated on the steps of the capital, even though demonstrations were forebidden. _____

6. Conpensation will be given to people enjured on the job pervided all enstructions are followed. _____

7. The interductory driver's education class does endeed teach intrastate driving for travel between states. _____

8. She pleaded for tolerence when I visited her after she had become a victum of violance. _____

9. Although Rudolph is very logicle and practicle, his superviser is inconsistant. _____

10. What an outragous hat you're wearing! Did you get it from a monkeys cage? _____

11. All senator-elects will meet with the vice presidents assistant in chambers. _____

12. The meeting of attorney generals and solicitor generals as well as their runner-ups and other delegate's will now convene. _____

13. Thiefs broke into my house and stole several CD's, two radioes, and my prize banjoes. _____

14. Several crisises have occured, creating a wish that I had more than two foots on the bottom of me legs. _____

WORD STUDIES

Review of Part I

Directions: Read the word in the first column; then (1) rewrite the word according to syllables in the second column and (2) indicate the word's primary part(s) of speech in the third column. If the word has two pronunciations, place the accent marks after the appropriate syllables in the second column and indicate all parts of speech in the third column. Use your dictionary as needed. On the blank line following each word, write a sentence using the word in which it is clearly defined.

Word	Syllabication	Part(s) of Speech
1. addict		
2. atrophy		
3. bailiff		
4. convert		
5. estimate		
6. glaucoma		
7. impersonate		
8. languishing		
9. permit		
10. plentiful		
11. purification		
12. recapitulate		
13. separate		
14. toilsome		
15. underachiever		

Review of Part 2

Directions: *Each sentence contains several sets of words in parentheses. Read the sentence; then circle the correct spelling of the word in parentheses.*

1. The (by stander/by-stander/bystander) who witnessed the crime couldn't speak fluent English and required a (go between/go-between/gobetween) to answer the questions posed by the (attorney at law/attorney-at-law).

2. Although he claims to be a (self made/self-made/selfmade) man, he has yet to (sucede/succeed/susede) at any job for which he's (excedingly/exceedingly/exsedeingly) qualified.

3. The (fotograph/photograph) showed three (delightful/delitful) girls standing in front of a (chalk board/chalk-board/chalkboard) displaying the (alfabet/alphabet).

4. Vast (improvement/improvment) has been seen in your (continueing/continuing) efforts to master (tieing/tying) your shoes.

5. (Paid/Payed) attendance at the movie showing the (betrayal/betraial) of the (armies/armys) was very (tring/trying) and disappointing.

6. The (leiutenant/lieutenant)'s (greif/grief) was unbearable as the army (seized/siezed) his homeland.

7. Mother was never afraid to get plenty of (protein/protien) in our (deit/diet). She'd (forfeit/forfiet) empty (caloreis/calories) for solid (nutreints/nutrients).

8. The order was (shiped/shipped) before the postal (personel/personnel) (recomended/reccommended/recommended) instituting a tracer.

9. Although Mr. Best (authored/authorred) the article, Ms. Swanson (edited/editted) it and (submited/submitted) it for publication.

10. A (satisfying/satisfing) (expereince/experience) for people with (creattive/creative) minds is to (interveiw/interview) the university resident poet.

WORD STUDIES

Review of Part 3

Directions: *Using contextual clues, determine the correct prefix from the list at the left of each sentence. Then on the blank line preceding each word root, write the prefix to complete the meaning of the sentence.*

1. ante/anti   Prescribed medicine containing _____ bodies was given through an IV to correct the baby's _____ natal condition caused by the _____ histamine used by the mother during pregnancy.

2. for/fore   _____ ever is such a long time. Unless we can meet in the _____ noon, I'll likely _____ get you.

3. com/con/co/col/cor   What a _____ incidence! Two vehicles _____ lided precisely as the press _____ ference to _____ rect traffic problems _____ menced.

4. de/dis/di/dif   Josh _____ gressed from his assigned topic as he _____ emphasized the _____ ferent public _____ plays in the museum.

5. em/en/im/in/il/ir   During your _____ vestigation, if you _____ counter any _____ valid, _____ legal, or _____ rational explanations, make all necessary corrections to avoid _____ barrassing yourself with less than _____ peccable conclusions.

6. inter/intro/intra   Sergio was recruited from the school's _____ mural soccer team and was asked to _____ duce his kicking skills to the _____ collegiate football coaches.

7. per/pre/pro   Take all facts into _____ per _____ spective before _____ ceeding to make any biased _____ sumptions.

8. non/un   We never set out to be a _____ profit organization, but _____ fortunately our revenues have been _____ satisfactory.

9. sub/super/suc/suf/sug/sup/sus   Jan _____ gests you _____ impose one transparency on top of another to achieve _____ ficient _____ cess and to gain audience _____ port for your presentation on the _____ pension of the _____ marine transportation system.

10. mono/bi/semi/tri   It's time for your _____ annual ophthalmologist's examination. What might you need this visit: a _____ cle for your right eye, _____ focals for distance and reading, or _____ focals for close work, reading, and distance?

11. hyper/hypo   People with high blood pressure, or _____ tension, are rarely cured with an injection of serum in a _____ dermic needle.

12. post/trans/up   The _____ portation Department has asked for _____ wards of $2 billion to repair the _____ earthquake destruction.

Review of Part 4

Directions: *Using contextual clues, determine the correct suffix from the list at the left of each sentence. Then on the blank line following each word root, write the suffix to complete the meaning of the sentence.*

1. able/ible   A depend_____ person is generally access_____ to those who need reli_____ assistance.

2. able/ible   If you are elig_____ for avail_____ and afford_____ housing, please complete all applic_____ lines on the enclosed application.

3. ant/ent   The brilli_____ applic_____ for the position of account_____ withdrew her application after the shouting incid_____.

4. ant/ent   Fraudul_____ scam artists prey on innoc_____ people with the int_____ of stealing their life savings.

5. ance/ence   Afflu_____ is no excuse for ill manners by people with little pati_____ and toler_____.

6. ance/ence   Attend_____ at the confer_____ is open to anyone who believes he or she can make a differ_____.

7. cal/cel/cle   Due to techni_____ difficulties, we must can_____ the vo_____ part of our classi_____ program at the Cir_____ Theater.

8. ar/er/or   My counsel_____'s office is on the fifty-fourth floor of the skyscrap _____. From the street, you need binocul_____s to see her office.

9. cian/tian   My college professor, a true academi_____, says a Mar_____ couldn't live in Earth's atmosphere.

10. sion/tion   Opposi_____ to an exten_____ of the exemp_____ of the restric_____ on the admis_____ of South American natives continually lobby Congress for preven_____ of these people's civil rights.

11. ary/ery/ory   I achieved a vict_____ when I correctly identified the myst_____ voice as that of our honor_____ mayor.

12. ise/ize/yze   Transportation was paral_____d when authorities with so-called expert_____ couldn't visual_____ the disgu_____d problem.

13. ous/eous   An anonym_____ donor made a spontan_____ donation of numer_____ valuable books to the fabul_____ collection at the city library.

14. ious/uous   Feeling conspic_____ before the large crowd, Mr. Secrist became anx_____, yet he remained grac_____ without being impet_____.

15. ee/er   The newly hired employ_____ acted in good taste, bringing commendation from her em-ploy_____.

WORD STUDIES

Review of Part 5

Directions: *On the blank line to the right of each sentence, rewrite the words in parentheses to make the correct plural or possessive form.*

1. The (book) and (supply) have arrived for next (year) academic courses.

2. Reviewing the football film, I noticed our (opponent) used three basic (blitz) in defensive coverage.

3. I find it difficult to keep up with the two (family) of (Jones) in our neighborhood. Now they're both building (patio) in their (backyard).

4. (Story) abound concerning the (company) downfall, although I understand the company failed because of decreasing (revenue).

5. Feeling as conspicuous as (monkey) in a zoo, we opened the (car) (door) and stepped out to prove we weren't injured.

6. If you can set the table with (dish), (fork), (spoon), and (knife), you'll reduce my (wife) burden.

7. When the twin (piano) start playing, the (alto) and (soprano) will sing; the (tenor) will hum the melody to simulate sounds of (echo).

8. (Winner) will receive gold (medal); (runner-up) will receive (certificate of entry) containing (notary public) seals.

9. (Child) need to take care of their (tooth) to avoid (cavity).

10. The (syllabus) containing the (datum) on proposed (curriculum) changes in (Appendix) A and B will be distributed, along with (thesis) statements by the (author).

11. (Proceeds) from the charity sale will be given to the United Way for distribution to needy (man) and (woman).

12. (Stockholder) equity will be paid either at the (stock) maturity or when the stock is sold by the (owner).

13. The (coach) and (assistant coach) (office) of the (man) baseball team are located on the second floor.

14. (Tim and Julie) house contains many (built-in) in the modern style of (furnishing).

Review of Part 6

Directions: *Each of the sentences contains two or more underlined words. On the first blank line, rewrite the sentence using synonyms for the underlined words. On the second blank line, rewrite the sentence using antonyms for the underlined words.*

1. Please <u>pay</u> your bill <u>promptly</u>.

   (syn.) _____

   (ant.) _____

2. Your <u>antics</u> greatly <u>amuse</u> me.

   (syn.) _____

   (ant.) _____

3. Hector is an <u>honest</u> person who can be <u>depended</u> upon.

   (syn.) _____

   (ant.) _____

4. Anne Marie is a <u>young</u>-<u>looking</u> <u>beauty</u>.

   (syn.) _____

   (ant.) _____

5. My husband <u>receives</u> a <u>modest</u> income each pay period.

   (syn.) _____

   (ant.) _____

6. Joan is an <u>excellent</u> <u>worker</u>, always submitting her work on <u>time</u>.

   (syn.) _____

   (ant.) _____

7. My <u>boss</u> is so <u>conservative</u> he <u>thinks</u> his employees' time is his own.

   (syn.) _____

   (ant.) _____

8. <u>Peace</u> began to <u>settle</u> in the valley following the <u>devastating</u> earthquake.

   (syn.) _____

   (ant.) _____

9. My attorney's <u>advice</u> is to <u>ignore</u> anyone <u>collecting</u> debts and to send collectors <u>directly</u> to her.

   (syn.) _____

   (ant.) _____

10. I am <u>happy</u> to <u>inform</u> you that your uncle left the <u>majority</u> of his estate to you.

    (syn.) _____

    (ant.) _____

11. I <u>see</u> you <u>took</u> my advice on building a <u>better</u> relationship with your wife.

    (syn.) _____

    (ant.) _____

12. What a <u>sad</u> face! Smile and <u>see</u> if the world looks <u>brighter</u>.

    (syn.) _____

    (ant.) _____

WORD STUDIES

Review of Spelling Words Correctly

Directions: *The column on the left lists the first and last letters of a previously reviewed spelling word. After reading the word's definition in the column on the right, write the remaining letters of the word on the blank line to spell the word correctly.*

1. a_____e   to make room for

2. a_____y   an organization that provides help

3. c_____r   a table showing months, weeks, and days

4. c_____r   a person who drives an automobile for another

5. c_____m   unfavorable remarks or judgments

6. e_____s   to make uneasy and ashamed

7. e_____n   a telephone connected to a main telephone

8. f_____r   well known; ordinary

9. g_____r   the study of the correct usage of words

10. h_____s   to trouble by repeated attacks

11. h_____s   an empty space from which something is missing

12. i_____e   to inject to prevent disease

13. l_____n   a connection between two units or people

14. l_____e   a paper showing permission to do something

15. m_____e   the act of supporting or keeping in existence

16. o_____e   to bind by a promise or contract

17. o_____n   a particular time; a special event

18. p_____r   out of the ordinary; strange

19. p_____e   a special right or advantage

20. q_____e   a printed list of questions to be answered

21. r_____d   to speak in favor of

22. s_____e   to divide from; distinct

23. s_____r   much the same; alike

24. t_____f   an excise tax placed on imported goods

25. v_____m   an empty space with no air

Review of Making Sense of Word Pairs

Directions: *In each of the following sentences, select the correct words from those given in parentheses. Write your choice from the first group of words on the first line to the right of the sentence (Choice A) and your choice from the second group on the second line (Choice B).*

	Choice A	Choice B
1. My (advice/advise) to you is to invest your (capital/capitol) funds in municipal bonds.	_____	_____
2. Last year's bill passed by the (legislator/legislature) has been a real (boom/boon) to this town.	_____	_____
3. I (council/counsel) you to (choose/chose) good friends who will support you.	_____	_____
4. At the group therapy session, (every one/everyone) (accept/except) Laura and Wilson participated.	_____	_____
5. Striding down the (bridal/bridle) path, Rachael's horse managed to (brake/break) loose, causing her to lose control.	_____	_____
6. The visiting dignitary (preceded/proceeded) down the aisle (passed/past) the approving audience.	_____	_____
7. If you want to (loose/lose) weight, get plenty of (lean/lien) foods in your diet.	_____	_____
8. "(Its/It's) (later/latter) than you think," the sage observed.	_____	_____
9. The city (ordinance/ordnance) and the (statue/stature/statute) signed by the governor both promote citizens' rights.	_____	_____
10. In his book's (foreword/forward), the author thanked his editor for the (role/roll) she played in the book's development.	_____	_____
11. As a result of the (collision/collusion), I have (continual/continuous) pain in my neck.	_____	_____
12. The new regulations will (affect/effect) (emigrants/immigrants) coming into the country.	_____	_____
13. With the layoff, management is forced to (sever/severe) (personal/personnel) employed less than a year.	_____	_____
14. Lu's (principal/principle) attribute is his ability to (complement/compliment) others on their good work.	_____	_____
15. In my term paper, I (cite/sight/site) the person who was declared (illegible/ineligible) after winning the race.	_____	_____

WORD STUDIES

Review of Business-Related Terminology

Directions: *Each numbered item contains the definition of a business-related term previously studied followed by three business-related terms. Read each definition; then circle the term that is defined.*

1. a charge for the use of credit   credit/earnest money/finance charge

2. the lowest interest rate on business loans   interest/prime rate/variance

3. the inability to pay one's debts   foreclosure/insolvency/liquidity

4. efforts to overcome problems in hiring women and minorities
   affirmative action/discrimination/equal opportunity

5. down payment given in good faith for binding a contract   earnest money/receivable/remuneration

6. the placement of funds given to a third party   compensation/escrow/guarantee

7. the person who receives the proceeds of a policy after the death of the policyholder
   adjuster/beneficiary/clientele

8. legal contracts indicating debts payable in money before maturity of debt
   contract/mortgage/negotiable instrument

9. the process by which an insurance company determines if it will accept an applicant for insurance
   coinsurance/prorate/underwriting

10. an asset a borrower pledges as security   collateral/equity/premium

11. an official document ordering a person to court   garnishment/indictment/subpoena

12. a legal instrument that transfers title of property   certificate of deposit/deed/deposition

13. a document made during an owner's lifetime that stipulates succession of the owner's income
    intestate/living trust/probate

14. a law requiring creditors to state monthly and annual percentage rates used as finance charges
    credit/disclosure statement/truth in lending

15. one having the authority to act in the name of another   civil rights/joint tenancy/proxy

16. money or something that grows in value   accrual/fringe benefit/per diem

17. a decrease in value due to age, wear, etc.   amortization/depreciation/stagnation

18. a sharp increase in prices resulting from too great an increase in money or bank credit
    deflation/inflation/recession

19. the amount of money obtained from the sale of goods or services   debit/dividends/proceeds

20. a tax-deductible expense caused by an uncollected debt or bad investment
    encumbrance/liability/write-off

Review of Computer-Related Terminology

Directions: *Each numbered item contains the definition of a computer-related term previously studied followed by three computer-related terms. Read each definition; then circle the term that is defined.*

1. the process of finding errors in a program   debugging/decoding/programming

2. the capability of moving from one system to another   compatibility/portability/protocol

3. a computer that can be carried   laptop/distributed processing/platform

4. the location of data on a floppy or hard disk   address/I/O/network

5. the study of the human factors related to computing   ergonomics/hypermedia/multitasking

6. material stored as a unit on a disk   configuration/file/map

7. a computer software program   application/transparent/update

8. handheld device for inputting data   digitizer/file server/mouse

9. a user's area consisting of a computer and peripherals   architecture/backbone/workstation

10. mail sent, received, and stored using the computer   electronic filing/electronic mail/sorting

11. the settings obtained upon retrieving a program   boot/default/initialize

12. the location where a new product is tested   beta site/screen dump/vendor

13. the speed at which information flows between devices   baud/bit/refresh

14. similar in architecture as another system   clone/LAN manager/protocol

15. a license granting multiple copies of software to be used at one location
    addressability/documentation/site license

16. a numbering system composed of ones and zeros   asynchronous/bar code/binary

17. the process of sending files from a mainframe to a personal computer   abort/access/download

18. the available RAM in a computer   buffer/memory/memory resident

19. the volatile memory in a computer   BIOS/RAM/ROM

20. adapted to make a program easy to use   computer-assisted/menu-driven/user-friendly

REFERENCES

Proofreader Marks   130

Summary of Spelling Rules   131

Commonly Used Prefixes   133

Commonly Used Suffixes   135

Proofreader Marks

Function	Symbol	Example	Final Copy
Align copy.	‖	‖Losses and revenues	Losses and revenues
Begin new paragraph.	¶	¶ The first line and the second line are	The first line and the second line are
Capitalize.	≡	san diego	San Diego
Close up space.	⌒	per cent	percent
Delete.	ℰ	omit that this	omit this
Delete and close up space.	ℰ	non-taxable	nontaxable
Insert.	∧	put *this* in	put this in
Insert apostrophe.	∨	peoples party	people's party
Insert brackets.	[/]	principle amount [sic]	principle amount [*sic*]
Insert colon.	⸪	the following	the following:
Insert comma.	∧	lions, tigers and monkeys	lions, tigers, and monkeys
Insert diagonal.	∅	and/or employed	and/or employed
Insert hyphen.	=/	up/to/date report	up-to-date report
Insert period.	⊙	the end	the end.
Insert quotation marks.	∨	It said, Ouch!	It said, "Ouch!"
Insert semicolon.	∧	May 20, 1999	May 20, 1999;
Insert space.	#	squaredance	square dance
Let it stand.	(stet)	frequently used (stet)	frequently used
Lowercase.	/	on the East side	on the east side
Make italic.	—	Rule 3	*Rule 3*
Move down.	⊔	degree	degree
Move left.	⊏	⌐Paragraph	Paragraph
Move right.	⊐	Indention⌐	Indention
Move up.	⊓	subscript	subscript
Spell out.	(SP)	30% (SP)	30 percent
Straighten the line.	═	straighten the line	straighten the line
Transpose.	tr ∿	to finish start	start to finish

Summary of Spelling Rules

The following summary outlines the spelling rules presented in this text. The page reference is given in parentheses following each rule.

RULE 1. Words Ending in Silent *e*.
(a) When words end in silent *e* and are preceded by a consonant, retain the *e* when adding a suffix beginning with a consonant. (b) When words end in silent *e* and are preceded by a consonant, drop the *e* when adding a suffix beginning with a vowel. (c) When words end in silent *e* and are preceded by the vowel *o*, retain the final *e* when adding the suffix *-ing*. (d) When words end in *ce* with the *c* sounding like *s* or *z*, and when words end in *ge* with the *g* sounding like *j*, generally retain the final *e*. (p. 24)

RULE 2. Words Ending in *ie*.
When words end in *ie*, drop the *e* and change the *i* to *y* when adding the suffix *-ing*. (p. 24)

RULE 3. Words Ending in *y* Preceded by a Consonant.
(a) When words end in *y* and are preceded by a consonant, generally change the *y* to *i* and add the suffix. (b) When the suffix begins with *i*, the *y* is generally retained. (c) When the suffix *s* is added to the root word and the *y* is changed to *i*, the suffix is generally spelled *-ies*. (p. 25)

RULE 4. Words Ending in *y* Preceded by a Vowel.
When words end in *y* and are preceded by a vowel, the *y* is retained when the suffix is added. Irregular verbs do not follow this rule. (p. 25)

RULE 5. The *ei* and *ie* Sequences.
When *e* and *i* occur together in a word, the *i* generally precedes the *e* except in the following circumstances: (a) when the sound of long *e* follows *c*, (b) when the two vowels are pronounced as long *a*, (c) when the two vowels are pronounced as long *i*, (d) when the two vowels are pronounced as short *i* following *f*, and (e) when the word begins with these two letters. (p. 27)

RULE 6. Suffixes: One-Syllable Words Ending in a Consonant.
When a one-syllable word ends in a consonant preceded by a vowel, double the consonant if the suffix begins with a vowel. Do not double the consonant if the suffix begins with a consonant. (p. 63)

RULE 7. Suffixes: Two-Syllable Words Ending in a Consonant.
When a suffix beginning with a vowel is added to a two-syllable word ending in a single consonant preceded by a single *accented* vowel, the final consonant is doubled. The final consonant is not doubled, however, if the new word does not retain the same accent as the root word. (p. 64)

RULE 8. Suffixes: Words Ending in *e*.
When a word ends in *e*, the *e* is retained before a suffix beginning with a consonant. The *e* is dropped before a suffix beginning with a vowel. (p. 65)

RULE 9. Suffixes: Words Ending in *y*.
When a word ends in *y* preceded by a consonant, change the *y* to *i* on the addition of all suffixes except those beginning with *i*. Retain the *y* before suffixes beginning with *i*. When a word ends in *y* preceded by a vowel, retain the *y* when adding a suffix. (p. 66)

RULE 10. Plural Forms: Most Nouns.
Most nouns form their plurals by adding *s*. (p. 87)

RULE 11. Plural Forms: Nouns Ending in *s, x, z, ch, sh*, and *ss*.
Nouns ending in *s, x, z, ch, sh*, and *ss* form their plurals by adding *es*. (p. 87)

RULE 12. Plural Forms: Proper Nouns.
Proper nouns form their plurals in the same manner as common nouns. An *s* is added to most proper nouns; but an *es* is added to proper nouns ending in *s, x, z, ch, sh*, and *ss*. (p. 87)

RULE 13. Plural Forms: Nouns Ending in *y* Preceded by a Consonant.
Nouns ending in *y* preceded by a consonant form their plurals by changing the *y* to *i* and adding *es*. (p. 88)

RULE 14. Plural Forms: Nouns Ending in y Preceded by a Vowel.
Nouns ending in *y* preceded by a vowel form their plurals by adding *s*. (p. 88)

RULE 15.   Plural Forms: Nouns Ending in *f* and *fe*.

Most nouns ending in *f* and *fe* form their plurals by adding *s*. Some nouns, however, form their plurals by changing the *f* to *v* and adding *es*. (p. 88)

RULE 16.   Nouns Ending in *o*.

The plural of nouns ending in *o* preceded by a vowel is generally formed by adding *s*. The plural of most nouns ending in *o* preceded by a consonant is often formed by adding *es*. Nouns ending in *o* that are related to music form their plurals by adding *s*. (p. 89)

RULE 17.   Plural Forms: Compound Nouns.

Hyphenated compound nouns and unhyphenated compound nouns are composed of two or more words but are considered as one word. These nouns form their plurals by adding *s* to the principal word. Compound nouns written as one word usually form their plurals by adding *s* to the end. When an adverb or a preposition is hyphenated as part of a compound noun, the plural is formed by adding *s* to the noun unless the adverb or the preposition is the dominant word. (p. 89)

RULE 18.   Plural Forms: Letters, Signs, and Symbols.

The plural of a lowercase letter, number, sign, or symbol is typically formed by adding an apostrophe and an *s*. Plurals of uppercase letters generally do not include an apostrophe. (p. 89)

RULE 19.   Plural Forms: Irregular Nouns.

Irregular nouns form their plurals through structural changes within the word. (p. 90)

RULE 20.   Plural Forms: Foreign Nouns.

Foreign nouns that do not use an English spelling form their plurals by changing the final letter or letters as indicated: (a) *a* changes to *ae*, (b) *us* changes to *i*, (c) *is* changes to *es*, (d) *eau* changes to *eaux*, (e) *um* changes to *a*, (f) *on* changes to *a*, (g) *ix* and *ex* change to *ces*, and (h) *o* changes to *i*. (p. 90)

RULE 21.   Singular Nouns.

Regardless of their spelling, some nouns are always singular in use. (p. 91)

RULE 22.   Plural Nouns.

Regardless of their spelling, some nouns are always plural in use. (p. 91)

RULE 23.   Same Form for Singular and Plural.

Some nouns use the same spelling for both the singular and the plural forms. (p. 91)

RULE 24.   Collective Nouns.

Collective nouns are singular in form but refer to a group of persons or things. When the context of the sentence indicates the group is acting as a whole, the collective noun takes a singular verb. When the context emphasizes the individual members of the group, the collective noun takes a plural verb. (p. 91)

RULE 25.   Possessives: Nouns Not Ending in *s*.

Nouns not ending in *s* form their possessives by adding an apostrophe and an *s*. (p. 92)

RULE 26.   Possessives: Singular Nouns Ending in *s*.

Singular nouns of one syllable ending in the sound of *s* generally form their possessives by adding an apostrophe and an *s*. Singular nouns of more than one syllable ending in the sound of *s* generally form their possessives by adding an apostrophe only. (p. 92)

RULE 27.   Plural Nouns Ending in *s*.

Plural nouns ending in *s* form their possessives by adding an apostrophe only. (p. 92)

RULE 28.   Possessives: Compound Nouns.

Compound nouns form their possessives by adding an apostrophe and an *s* to the final word. (p. 93)

RULE 29.   Possessives: Joint and Separate Ownership.

Joint ownership is indicated by adding an apostrophe and an *s* to the last noun of the two-or-more noun combination. Separate ownership is indicated by making each noun possessive. (p. 93)

RULE 30.   Possessives: Pronouns.

Pronouns form their possessives through irregular spelling changes. An apostrophe is never used in the possessives of pronouns. (p. 93)

WORD STUDIES

Commonly Used Prefixes

Prefix	Prefix Meaning	Examples of Usage
1. a-	in, on, to, off, in the act of	abroad, asleep, away
2. ab- (a-, abs-)	away, from, off	abnormal, absent, abstract
3. ad- (a-, ac-, af-, ag-, al-, an-, ap-, ar-, as-, at-)	to, toward, at	adhere, admit, accompany
4. ante-	before, in front of	antedate, antecedent, anteroom
5. anti- (ant-)	against, not, opposite	antibody, antifreeze, anti-American
6. apo- (ap-)	from, away, separate	apology, apostrophe, apostate
7. arch- (arche-, archi-)	chief, extreme	archbishop, architect, archenemy
8. bi-	twice a, occurring every two	biannual, biweekly, bisect
9. cata- (cat-)	down, against	catabolism, catalyst, category
10. circum-	in a circle, around	circumnavigate, circumstance
11. com- (co-, col-, con-, cor-)	with, together, altogether	compare, coexist, collect, contain, correlate
12. contra- (contro-, counter-)	against, in opposition	contradict, counteract, contraband
13. de-	do opposite of, down, remove	decrease, depress, deemphasize
14. di-	twice, double, twofold	digraph, dioxide, dichotomy
15. dia- (di-)	through, across, thoroughly	diagonal, diagram, diaphragm
16. dis- (di-, dif-)	not, opposite of	dishonest, divert, different
17. en- (em-)	make, in, on, cause to be	enable, employ, enthrone
18. epi- (ep-)	on, upon, above, among	epitaph, epidemic, epidermis
19. ex- (e-, ef-)	former, out of, from	ex-president, exit, effluent
20. extra- (extro-)	outside, beyond	extraordinary, extravagant
21. for-	away, opposite, completely	forbid, forgive, forsake
22. fore-	front, before	forearm, foreground, forecast
23. hyper-	over, above, exceedingly	hyperactive, hypertension
24. hypo-	under, beneath, below	hypocrite, hypodermic, hypothermia

Prefix	Prefix Meaning	Examples of Usage
25. in- (il-, im-, ir-, en-)	in, into, not, within	insert, immodest, illegible
26. inter-	one with the other, between	interact, intercede, interview
27. intra-	within, inside	intramural, intrastate, intraparty
28. intro-	inward, within	introvert, introduce, introspect
29. meta- (met-)	among, change of place/state	metamorphosis, metabolize
30. mis-	wrongly, badly	misbehave, mismanagement, miscue
31. non-	not, opposite of, lack of	noncommissioned, nonessential
32. ob- (o-, oc-, of-, op-, os-)	against, contrary, toward	opposite, ostracize, obstacle, omit, occasion, offend
33. par- (para-)	beside, near, defense against	paramedic, parable, parachute
34. per-	throughout, thoroughly	perceive, perfection, perforate
35. peri-	around, surrounding, near	perimeter, periscope, perigee
36. post-	after, later, behind	postwar, postdate, posterior
37. pre-	before, in front of	predate, prearrange, precaution
38. pro-	forward, on the side of, before	project, pro-American, produce
39. re-	again, back	react, rebroadcast, repay
40. retro-	backward	retroactive, retrofire, retrograde
41. semi-	half, partly	semiannual, semicircle, semiskilled
42. sub- (suc-, suf-, sug-, sup-, sus-)	under, down, again	submarine, suggest, sustain
43. super- (sur-)	over, above, besides	supervise, superfluous, superior
44. sym- (syn-)	together, with, at the same time	symbolize, synonym
45. trans-	across, over, beyond	transaction, transatlantic
46. ultra-	beyond, very	ultrasonic, ultraviolet, ultrasound
47. un-	not, opposite of	unaffected, unbiased, uncertain
48. up-	up, toward the top of, through	upbringing, update

Commonly Used Suffixes

Suffix	Suffix Meaning	Examples of Usage
1. -able (-ible, -ble)	able to be, suitable for, that can be	breakable, feasible, feeble
2. -age	act of, group of, condition of	storage, breakage, bondage
3. -al (-ial)	of, like, having nature of, act of	arrival, fictional, facial
4. -an (-ian)	having to do with, from, skilled in	Freudian, American, historian
5. -ance (-ancy)	act or fact of, state of, thing that	performance, reliance, buoyancy
6. -ant (-ent)	one that is, that does something	assistant, reluctant, president
7. -ar	of or having to do with	popular, columnar, regular
8. -arian	one who believes in	disciplinarian, librarian
9. -ary	place for, collection of, person that	infirmary, vocabulary, notary
10. -ate	become, having to do with, containing	maturate, collegiate, compassionate
11. -cy	office or rank of, fact of being	bankruptcy, accuracy, solvency
12. -dom	position, rank of, condition of being	kingdom, boredom, freedom
13. -ed	having characteristics of	edited, dressed, confessed
14. -ee	person who is	employee, mortgagee, appointee
15. -eer	person who directs, deals with	volunteer, auctioneer, electioneer
16. -en	cause to be, become, made of	liken, thicken, wooden
17. -ence (-ency)	condition of being, act or fact of	dependence, difference, frequency
18. -eous	having the nature of, like	gaseous, beauteous, courteous
19. -er (-or)	person or thing connected with	rancher, carpenter, governor
20. -ery (-ry)	place for, art of, condition of	cookery, slavery, scenery
21. -ese	having to do with, native or language of	legalese, Japanese, Chinese
22. -esque	in the style of	Romanesque, picturesque
23. -est	most	hottest, slowest, loveliest
24. -et (-ette)	little	kitchenette, islet, booklet
25. -ful	full of, showing, having tendency to	helpful, eventful, harmful
26. -fy	make, cause to be, become	satisfy, simplify, ratify
27. -hood	state of being, group of, nature of	childhood, statehood, falsehood
28. -ic (-ical)	having to do with, having nature of	artistic, heroic, biblical
29. -ier (-yer)	person concerned with	clothier, cashier, lawyer
30. -ine (-in)	like, like that of	chlorine, equine, canine
31. -ing (-ings)	act that, result	running, lasting, feelings

	Suffix	Suffix Meaning	Examples of Usage
32.	-ion, (-sion, -tion)	act of, condition of, result of	confession, expulsion, description
33.	-ish	somewhat, like, inclined to be	devilish, childish, bookish
34.	-ism	act or practice of, quality or condition	criticism, paganism, alcoholism
35.	-ist	person who, expert, one engaged in	florist, tourist, organist
36.	-ite	descendant of, fossil, mineral	Israelite, sulphite, graphite
37.	-itis	inflammation of, disease of	appendicitis, bronchitis
38.	-ity (-ty)	quality of condition, fact of being	sincerity, possibility, safety
39.	-ive	of or having to do with, likely to	possessive, active, initiative
40.	-ize (-ise, -yze)	make, engage in, become	paradise, criticize, paralyze
41.	-less	without, does not, cannot be	careless, thoughtless, meaningless
42.	-let	little, thing worn as a band	booklet, ringlet, anklet
43.	-like	like a, like	lifelike, childlike, snaillike
44.	-ling	little, unimportant, one belonging to	suckling, groundling, buckling
45.	-ly	in a manner, to a degree, like a	carefully, slowly, quickly
46.	-ment	act or fact of, condition of, means of	payment, bewilderment, enticement
47.	-most	greatest in amount, degree, number	foremost, utmost, topmost
48.	-ness	quality of being, behavior	kindness, carefulness, whiteness
49.	-oid	like, thing like a	spheroid, humanoid, asteroid
50.	-ory	involving, tending to, place for	preparatory, factory, illusory
51.	-osis	act or process of, abnormal condition	osmosis, cirrhosis, neurosis
52.	-ous	full of, nature of, involving	famous, rigorous, polygamous
53.	-ry	occupation, condition of, group of	ministry, rivalry, citizenry
54.	-ship	office of, condition of, skill of	senatorship, friendship, seamanship
55.	-some	tending to, causing, to a great degree	bothersome, troublesome, wholesome
56.	-ster	one who makes	youngster, jokester, mobster
57.	-ule	small	lobule, ampule, capsule
58.	-ure	act of, state of, something that	seizure, pleasure, lecture
59.	-ward (-wards)	in the direction of, toward	backwards, outward, seaward
60.	-wise	in a manner, in the characteristic way of, in the direction of	clockwise, likewise, computerwise
61.	-y (-ie)	small, full of, having, inclined to, resembling, quality of being	doggie, risky, salty, choosy, sketchy

WORD STUDIES